What To Do For Senior Health

Easy to Read • Easy to Use

Albert Barnett, M.D.
Nancy Rushton, R.N.

Institute for Healthcare Advancement
501 S. Idaho St., Suite 300
La Habra, California 90631

© 2015 by Institute for Healthcare Advancement
501 S. Idaho St., Suite 300
La Habra, California 90631
(800) 434-4633

Printed in the United States of America
15 14 13   8 7 6 5
ISBN: 978-0-9701245-4-8

To Our Readers

Seniors today are living longer and healthier lives than ever before. Like most other seniors, you want to stay active and take care of yourself. You also want the best healthcare at a price you can afford.

If you want to take charge of your health, this book is for you. It gives tips on how to:

- Get good healthcare
- Handle normal changes
- Handle common health problems
- Stay well each day
- Stay safe
- Pay for healthcare
- Prepare for your future

How to use this book

You can read this book cover to cover. Or you can flip to sections you want to read about. Turn to page 3 to see what's inside.

As you read this book, you may want to write down facts, ideas, and questions. There is a place to take notes at the start of each section.

Be sure to write down your contacts on page 6.
And write about your health on page 9.

To Our Readers

Not sure what a word means? Turn to the word list on page 167. It gives the meanings of some words in the book.

Keep this book in a place where it is easy to find. And share it with your friends and family.

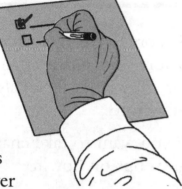

In some parts of the book you are asked questions about lists of things. For example, on page 55 you are asked if you take any of the over-the-counter medicines listed. Put a checkmark in the box to answer the question. Then read what to do next. Most of the time it will suggest that you share this information with your doctor.

This book is for you if:

- You are 50 or older
- You take care of a senior
- You want to know more about staying healthy as you get older

It was reviewed by doctors, nurses, and others who know a lot about healthcare for seniors. But it does not take the place of healthcare. If you have any health problems or questions about your health, please see your doctor.

What's Inside

What's Inside

What's Inside

My Contacts

Fill in this list of contact facts. Keep it handy.

Date I wrote this: _____

Medical emergency phone: **911** or _____

Fire emergency phone: **911** or _____

Police emergency phone: **911** or _____

Health insurance company name: _____

    Phone: _____

    Address: _____

    Email address or website: _____

    Hours: _____

Primary Care Doctor name: _____

    Phone: _____

    Address: _____

    Email address or website: _____

    Hours: _____

Doctor name: _____

    Phone: _____

    Address: _____

    Email address or website: _____

    Hours: _____

My Contacts

Doctor name: _____

    Phone: _____

    Address: _____

    Email address or website: _____

    Hours: _____

Dentist name: _____

    Phone: _____

    Address: _____

    Email address or website: _____

    Hours: _____

Eye doctor name: _____

    Phone: _____

    Address: _____

    Email address or website: _____

    Hours: _____

Urgent care center name: _____

    Phone: _____

    Address: _____

    Email address or website: _____

    Hours: _____

Hospital name: _____

    Phone: _____

    Address: _____

    Email address or website: _____

My Contacts

Pharmacy name: _____

    Phone: _____

    Address: _____

    Email address or website: _____

    Hours: _____

Lab name: _____

    Phone: _____

    Address: _____

    Email address or website: _____

    Hours: _____

Neighbor name: _____

    Phone: _____

Family member name: _____

    Phone: _____

Family member name: _____

    Phone: _____

Other phone numbers:

Name: _____ Phone: _____

Name: _____ Phone: _____

Name: _____ Phone: _____

Name: _____ Phone: _____

Name: _____ Phone: _____

My Health

Fill in this list of facts about your health. Keep it handy.

Allergies: _____

_____

_____

_____

_____

Health problems: _____

_____

_____

_____

_____

_____

_____

_____

_____

❏ I have an advance directive.

I keep it here: _____

(If you don't have an advance directive, see page 60. You can also go online to prepareforyourcare.org to make one.)

Staying Safe

People of all ages should think about safety. But it's a special concern for seniors. As you get older, you are more likely to fall, have a car crash, or get cheated by a scam.

Notes

_____

_____

_____

_____

_____

_____

_____

_____

_____

_____

_____

_____

_____

11

Prevent Falls

As you get older, you are more likely to fall down and get hurt. Each year, 1 out of 3 adults age 65 or older falls down. Falls are the top cause of injury for seniors.

That's because you are more likely to:

- Get dizzy
- Have trouble with your balance
- Get up during the night
- Have stiff joints
- Have trouble seeing
- Take medicines that make you weak, shaky, or sleepy

How to prevent falls

Keep a cell phone in your pocket or nearby. That way, you can call for help if you fall.

Limit how much you carry. The extra weight can make you lose your balance. If you are carrying bags in from the car, carry one bag at a time. Make extra trips if you have a lot to carry.

Stay active. If you are healthy, you will be less likely to fall.

Exercise to keep your muscles strong.

Talk to your doctor about mixing alcohol and medicines. Take extra care when you drink alcohol or take medicines that make you weak, shaky, or sleepy.

Wear safe shoes. Make sure they fit well and have low heels. The soles should grip well. Avoid wearing loose slippers, even in the house.

Wear your glasses. Wear your glasses, so you can see where you're going. Have your eyes checked and glasses checked once a year.

Ask your doctor if you need to use a cane or a walker. Use your cane or walker to help with your balance.

Avoid climbing on ladders. Store things you use a lot where you can reach them easily. If you have trouble reaching something, use a step stool. Stand in the middle of each step. Make sure the stool sits flat on the ground and has a handgrip. If you get dizzy on a step stool, ask someone to help you reach the item you need.

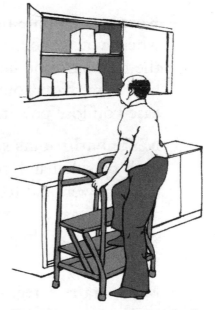

Use step stools with handrails.

Choose chairs that are easy to get up from. Make sure the seat is level, not too soft, not too low to the ground, and your feet touch the ground. Your back should rest against the back of the chair. The arms of the chair should be the length of your arms.

Prevent Falls

Get rid of clutter. That way, there will be less to trip over. Get rid of chairs and tables you don't need. Tie up cords. Get rid of loose throw rugs. Or put safety mats or tape under them. Never leave things on the stairs.

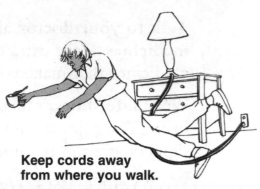

Keep cords away from where you walk.

Keep floors slip-free. Don't use floor wax. Wipe up any spills right away.

Keep outside walkways clear. Have someone clear away leaves, ice, and snow.

Keep your home bright. That way, you'll be able to see where you're going. Keep blinds and curtains open during the day. Turn on lights at night. Use night-lights in the bedroom, bathroom, and hall. Keep a flashlight handy in case you lose power.

Make bathrooms safer. Put grab bars or handgrips near the tub, shower, and toilet. Place a rubber mat in the tub and shower. Keep a night-light on all the time.

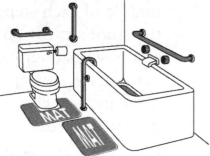

Make stairs safer. Keep them well lit. Put glow-in-the-dark tape on steps—even if there is just one step. Keep the railing in good shape, and always use it.

Prevent dizzy spells. Before you get out of bed, sit on the side of the bed for 10 seconds. Hold onto a table or dresser as you stand up.

Prevent falls outside

Avoid ice and uneven ground. If you must walk in these places, wear shoes that grip well. Hold onto someone. Use your cane or walker.

Beware of very hot weather. You may get dizzy and fall. Find a place with air conditioning. Drink plenty of water.

Watch out for single steps. Look down when you go into or out of a shop or restaurant. Look for uneven floors or concrete in the parking lot or on walkways.

Look first. Watch for things you might trip over, such as parking blocks in parking lots, or broken or uneven pavement.

Stay connected. Use an alert system. You push a button and it calls 911. Have someone call or check in on you once or twice a day.

Fall Safety Assessment

Check your risk for falling. Circle Yes or No for each statement below.

Statement	Yes	No
1. I have fallen in the last 6 months.	Yes = 2	No = 0
2. I use a cane or walker, or I have been told to use a cane or walker.	Yes = 2	No = 0
3. I feel unsteady sometimes when I am walking.	Yes = 1	No = 0
4. I hold onto furniture at home to steady myself.	Yes = 1	No = 0
5. I am worried about falling.	Yes = 1	No = 0
6. I need to push with my hands to stand up after sitting in a chair.	Yes = 1	No = 0
7. I have some trouble stepping up onto a curb.	Yes = 1	No = 0
8. I often have to rush to the toilet.	Yes = 1	No = 0
9. I have lost some feeling in my feet.	Yes = 1	No = 0
10. I take medicine that sometimes makes me feel light-headed or more tired than usual.	Yes = 1	No = 0
11. I take medicine to help me sleep or improve my mood.	Yes = 1	No = 0
12. I often feel sad or depressed.	Yes = 1	No = 0
Total Score		

Add up the number of points for each "Yes" answer. If your score is 4 or more, you may be at risk for falling. Talk to your doctor and your family about what you can do.

What to do if you fall

Stay still for a few moments. Take deep breaths to calm yourself.

Check to see if you are hurt. Slowly move your arms and legs. If you have bad pain in an arm, leg, neck, or hip, try not to move it.

If you can, turn onto your side. Try to push up to a sitting position. Then just sit for a few moments. Crawl to a sturdy chair, and pull yourself up.

Use a chair to pull yourself up after a fall.

Change position slowly. When you go from lying down to standing, or sitting to standing, wait a minute before walking. This gives your body time to adjust.

If you can't get up or have bad pain, call for help.

Call your doctor's office — tell them you had a fall, even if you don't think you're badly hurt.

Home Safety

Falls are not the only safety issue seniors need to think about. There are many things in your home that can harm you. Read this section carefully. Make notes. Talk about it with your loved ones. Talk about it with your doctor or nurse.

Stay safe from fire

Cook safely. Stay in the kitchen when the stove is on. Use a teapot that whistles or turns off when it's done. Use toasters and coffeemakers that turn off when they're done. Check the power cords on these items. If cords are bare, broken or frayed, replace the item. Use timers and notes to remind you to turn things off.

Don't smoke. If you do smoke, try to quit. Talk to your doctor. Or visit smokefree.gov. Until you quit, use ashtrays that don't tip over. Soak all cigarette and cigar butts with water before you throw them away. Never smoke in bed.

Heat your home safely. Keep space heaters 3 feet away from everything. Have your fireplace and chimney checked and cleaned each year. Never use the oven, open flames, or barbecue grills inside to heat your home.

Keep a fire extinguisher handy. Know how to use it. Have it checked once a year. Keep it close by and easy to reach.

Know what to do if there is a fire. Your top goal should be to get out of your home. If your clothes catch on fire, stop, drop, and roll until the flames are out.

Use electric blankets safely. Don't tuck in the edges. Don't put anything on top of the blanket. Never let pets sleep on top of or under an electric blanket. Don't eat or drink anything in bed.

Use smoke alarms. Put them in all bedrooms and the hallway. Change the batteries twice a year. To help you remember, change the batteries when you change your clocks and watches to and from Daylight Saving Time.

Stay safe from burns

Set your hot water heater to no higher than 120 degrees F (49 degrees C). And be careful when you use a microwave. The food and dish can get very hot.

Stay safe from poisons

Learn about carbon monoxide. It's an odorless gas that can kill you. Put carbon monoxide alarms in your kitchen and bedrooms. Never leave your car running in the garage—even for a minute.

Never mix cleaning products. If you mix them, you might make a poison gas that can burn or kill you.

Store poisons safely. Keep things such as cleaning products, bug sprays, and weed killers away from medicines. Keep them in the containers they came in. That way, you won't swallow them by mistake.

Stay safe from electricity

Keep electronics away from sinks and bathtubs so they won't fall in. And touch light switches and outlets only with dry hands.

Drive Safely

For many seniors, driving means freedom. It lets you go where you want, whenever you want. Plus, it may be easier than walking, riding a bike, or taking a bus.

But car crashes are among the top causes of death for seniors. That's because seniors may not see and hear as well as they used to. They may also move and react slower.

Get ready to drive

Choose your car wisely. Make sure you can see the road well. Think about getting a car with safety features such as a back-up camera.

Drive a car that lets you see the road well.

Have a cell phone with you. That way, you can call for help if you need it. But never text or talk while driving.

Have a hat and sunglasses with you. That way, you can put them on if the sun is in your eyes.

Keep your car in good shape. Make sure your headlights are clean. Make sure your windshield wipers work and have fluid.

Have your eyes checked once a year. Get new eyeglasses when your vision changes. Ask for coating on your lenses to cut glare.

Know where you are going. Read the directions, or set your GPS before you go. Know where to park.

Take a safe driving class. You'll learn something new. You may be charged less for car insurance.

Tell your doctor if you are having memory problems. Talk about driving and how to stay safe. If it is not safe for you to drive, ask where to get help.

Stay safe while driving

Wear a seat belt.

Always wear a seat belt. It could save your life.

Watch the road. Always pull over and stop in a safe spot before you eat, drink, use a cell phone, or change stations on the radio.

Drive in daylight. If you must drive at night, give your eyes time to get used to the dark. Don't look into the headlights of oncoming cars. Drive in the slow lane.

Drive in good weather. Stay off icy or wet roads. Avoid driving during a rainstorm or snowstorm.

Follow the speed limit. Don't drive too fast or too slow.

Leave plenty of space in front of your car. This will give you more time to react.

Limit turns. Avoid making U-turns and left turns. Change lanes only when you need to. Always use a turn signal when you turn or change lanes.

Pay attention. Watch out for people, cars, road signs, and traffic lights.

Know when NOT to drive

Do not drive if:

- You feel sleepy, dizzy, or sick
- You had even one drink of alcohol
- You take medicines that can make you sleepy or dizzy
- Your doctor says you should not drive

Want to drive less?

Try these options:

- Get home delivery for your medicines.
- Let a friend or family member do the driving.
- Pay bills online. Or set up automatic payments.
- See if there is a van service for seniors in your area.
- Shop online or by phone.
- Take a bus, train, or taxi.

Use home delivery services.

Elder Abuse

Elder abuse is harm that happens to a person who is 60 years of age and older. It usually happens to seniors who depend on and trust someone. Elder abuse usually takes place more than once, and can happen over and over again, to gain  control of a person. All seniors have legal rights. Elder abuse is a violation of human rights. Elder abuse is a crime.

Each year thousands of seniors are abused. Most of the people who are abused are 80 years or older. Elder abuse often happens to a person who is sick and frail. Elder abuse usually takes place when seniors are unable to take care of themselves. They need to have other people take care of their everyday needs. They may not be able to do their own banking or read their mail. The abuse is usually by a caregiver, family member, or another "trusted" person.

Elder abuse can take place in a senior's home, in a hospital, in a nursing home, in hospice, or any place where seniors live.

Here are some kinds of elder abuse:

- **Physical abuse.** Includes injury or harm by slapping, hitting, pushing, burning, kicking, or other abuse. The abuse may be to restrain a person, hold them down, or lock them in their room. It includes anything that is done with force to a senior. The abuse may cause bruises or broken bones. Or the abuser may be careful to not leave any marks.

- **Sexual abuse.** Forcing a senior to take part in a sex act without their consent.

- **Emotional abuse.** This harms a senior's emotional well-being or destroys their self-worth as a person. This includes many things:
  - Name calling
  - Saying or doing anything that embarrasses the senior or causes them to fear something.
  - Treating a senior like a child.
  - Taking away or destroying the things that belong to the senior.
  - Not allowing a senior to see their family or friends.

- **Neglect.** When someone responsible for the care of a senior does not provide food, housing, clothing, and medical care. Some signs include bed sores, or living conditions that are not clean or not safe. The senior may have lost a lot of weight.

- **Abandonment.** This is when a caregiver or another responsible person leaves the senior alone and no longer takes care of their daily needs.

- **Financial abuse or exploitation.** This is one of the most common forms of elder abuse. It's when another person illegally uses a senior's money, property, or anything else that the senior owns. Here are some signs that financial abuse may be happening:

  - Transfer of property to someone else
  - The elder is unable to pay their bills

- Items are missing from their home
- Heavy credit card use.

Many seniors suffer abuse in silence. They are afraid to call the police or tell friends or family about the abuse. It may be that the senior is afraid to let others know that they are being hurt by someone who takes care of them. Listen to a senior if they tell you that they are being abused. Get help for the person if you think they are being abused.

What to do if you think a senior is being abused.

When you think a senior's life is in danger, call 911 or the police. Tell them what you think is happening. That is all you need to do. You do not need to prove abuse. The police will look into the care of the senior.

When the senior is in an LTC (Long Term Care) facility you can talk to a Long Term Care Ombudsman about your concerns. Phone numbers for the Ombudsman are usually posted on a bulletin board in the building. If not, ask for the phone number at the desk.

Call Adult Protective Services in your community. Talk to them about what you think is happening with the senior. This is a confidential report.

Call the national Eldercare Locator at 1-800-677-1116 (on weekdays) or go to www.eldercare.gov. Talk to them about what you think is happening. They will know where to report the abuse. Your only job is to tell an agency about the elder abuse that you think is happening. Give them the information that they need. You do not need to help with an investigation.

What you can do so that elder abuse will not happen to you.

Plan ahead for your life as you age. Do not wait to plan. Decide where you want to live. (Read the chapter, "Deciding Where to Live" on page 68.) Decide who you want to help take care of your money, property, your healthcare, and any other matters, when you are unable to do so or when you die. Make your wishes known to family and friends. (Read the chapter, "How to Make Your Wishes Known" on page 60.) Have legal papers that tell who you want to sign legal documents for you and help you when

you are not able to take care of yourself. Legal help is available in most communities. Keep your legal papers up-to-date. Keep your legal papers in a safe place.

Get help with legal papers.

Elder Abuse

Be on your guard with family members who have money problems. Be careful when people ask you to change your will or add their name to your bank account. Before doing this, talk to a lawyer or a person that you can trust and who is outside of your family.

Spend time doing activities with other people. Keep strong relationships with family members and friends. Know people in your community. Have people visit you, even if only for a short time. Talk to them about your care and what your wishes are. Do not allow yourself to become lonely, cut off from others, left out, and without friends.

You have rights. Learn to "speak up" anytime you think you are being abused. Too many seniors remain silent.

For more information on elder abuse, go to the National Center on Elder Abuse website at ncea.aoa.gov.

Fraud and Scams

Seniors can be targets for criminals. As you grow older, you are more likely to be a victim of a crime. You may be less able to defend yourself. You need to be on your guard against crime. Thieves are very smart and clever. They know how to trick you to get what they want. Never be made to feel that you have to do something right now.

That could be a scam. A scam is a plan or an offer that is not honest. Other words for scam are fraud, swindle, trap, cheat, or trick.

It is better to ask for help. Think on it overnight or for a few days before signing papers or saying "yes." Do not be too trusting. Talk it over with someone you trust.

Identity theft

- Be very careful about giving your personal information to anyone. This includes people requesting it on the computer, over the phone, or a salesperson at your door. Your personal information includes your address, age, bank account number, and whether you live alone. Never give out your full Social Security number.

- Do not leave your name and address on papers you are throwing away. It is best to use a shredder for mail and important papers that you are throwing away and that have your name on them. You can also cut or tear your papers into small pieces.

- Do not leave your mail in a mailbox overnight.
- Check with your bank to learn which credit card you should use for everyday purchases and in restaurants. Only carry that one credit card with you when you are away from home.

Electronic computer, tablet, and phone safety

- Use passwords that contain 8 or more characters. This includes both small and capital letters, numbers, and characters like !#*. Do not use your name, the name of your dog, your birth date, or anything that identifies you. As an example: 854jlG330*. Change your passwords every 3 months.

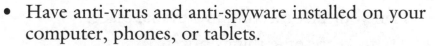

- Have anti-virus and anti-spyware installed on your computer, phones, or tablets.
- Install updates. Keep your operating system, anti-virus, anti-spyware, hardware, and software up-to-date.
- Only download items from a site that you know and trust. When looking for a website, make sure you are clicking on the exact site you want. Sometimes extra letters have been added to the name of a site. This may take you to a site set up by scammers.
- Only answer emails when you know who sent the email. Some emails look like they come from a company that you know, but they are fake. Before answering any email that you are not sure about, call their 800 number. Ask if they sent it to you.

- Beware of computer repair companies where you receive a call or notice on your computer or by a phone call. They may tell you that they work for a well-known company like Microsoft, but what they want is remote access to your computer. The sender or caller is only trying to get some of your personal information.

Request for money from charities

- Do not trust all charities that request money. Ask them to send you printed information about their charity. Ask other people about the charity before you give money.
- Unless you know the caller, hang up on any phone calls when they are asking for money. Don't worry about being rude.

Online Dating

- Remember that some people may not be honest with you.
- Take it slow.
- Plan your first meeting in a public place.
- Try to keep some things private.
- Be careful. Is the other person asking for anything other than friendship? Like money?

When you are out

- If you feel you are not safe, you probably are not safe. If someone or something makes you uneasy, trust your gut. Get to a safe place.
- It is always better to be with someone than to go out alone.
- Crimes can take place any time of day or night.

- Do not wear expensive jewelry or have other expensive items on you.

- Only carry a small amount of cash with you.

- Women with a purse should carry it close to their body. Men should not carry a wallet in a back pocket. Never set a purse or wallet down someplace, like in a grocery cart. Fanny packs are safer.

- Do not use an ATM that is in a hallway or a dark place.

- Have your car keys out and ready when going to your car. Lock your car doors, and keep your car doors locked. Keep your gas tank full. Do not keep packages and valuable items on your car seats.

Home repairs

- Beware of anything that is "free" or is a "discount."

- Do not feel you have to make a decision right away if you are not ready. Take time to check out the company and the price.

- Do not pay for services in advance.

- Get estimates and references on all home repairs. Ask how long they guarantee their work. Get it in writing.

- Ask your neighbors and other people about the company.

- Check out companies with the Better Business Bureau or Attorney General's Office.

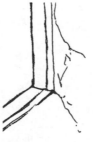

Fraud for seniors

- If it sounds too good to be true, it probably is.
- Scammers will try to talk you into giving them your personal information. Be careful, even if a person seems to be honest and someone you can trust. Scammers will be friendly with you just to get what they want.
- Sometimes to win a "prize" you must give out information about yourself or even money. Do not do this.
- Here are items where seniors need to be very careful: anti-aging products, funerals and cemetery sales, prescription drugs, investments, and reverse mortgages.

For more information

- National Crime Prevention Council at ncpc.org.
- FBI (Federal Bureau of Investigation) at fbi.gov/scams/fraud/seniors.

Getting Good Healthcare

2

Good healthcare from a doctor or other healthcare provider helps you stay healthy. It is important to find a doctor or other provider who gets to know you well, and who you trust. It is the best way to stay healthy. Your doctor and care team can help you learn about your health problems and get treatment for them.

Notes

_____

_____

_____

_____

_____

_____

_____

_____

_____

_____

_____

Know Ways to Get Healthcare

There are many ways to get healthcare, from your doctor's office to hospice care.

Doctor's office

Your doctor's office or clinic is the best place to meet most of your healthcare needs. Your doctor knows you and has your health records.

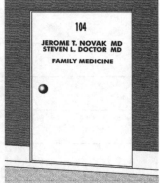

At your doctor's office, you can get:

- Yearly checkups
- Treatment for health problems that are not an emergency.
- Some tests
- Vaccines (shots)
- Answers to your questions

When you have a health concern, call your doctor right away. Don't wait. Small problems can become big problems or an emergency.

Urgent care center

These centers do most of the same things your doctor does. But they have longer hours. Many urgent care centers are open nights and weekends. Go here if you need to be seen right away but can't get in to your doctor.

You don't need to schedule a visit at an urgent care center. But you may need to wait as long as a few hours.

Surgery center

A surgery center is for surgery that can't be done in a doctor's office. In most cases, you can go home a few hours after surgery.

Before you have surgery, find out:

- If you need tests first
- How long before surgery you should stop eating and drinking
- When you should get to the surgery center
- How long you will have to stay
- If someone needs to drive you home
- What care you will need after surgery
- Whether the surgery center takes your insurance. Ask if they are in your network.

Hospital

You may get very sick or hurt and need hospital care. That means you stay overnight or longer in a hospital as an inpatient.

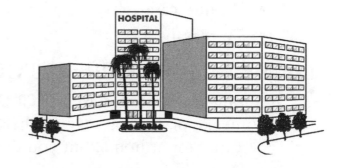

You may also get care in a hospital as an outpatient. That means you just visit the hospital for your care. You don't stay overnight. You may need this care to get x-rays, tests, or therapy.

Home healthcare

You may need care at home when you are too sick or weak to leave. Or you may need it when you have just left the hospital.

Most people need home healthcare and services for just a short time. A doctor must order the care. You can only get this care if you are unable to leave home.

Home healthcare may include:

- Equipment, such as wheelchairs and walkers
- Physical therapy, such as learning how to use crutches
- Shots
- Speech therapy, such as learning how to talk after a stroke
- Wound care
- IV therapy

Senior getting healthcare at home.

Long-term care facility (LTCF)

A long-term care facility (LTCF) provides care in a homelike place. You may go there when you are too sick to be cared for at home, but you don't need a hospital.

You may stay at an LTCF for a short time. Or you may live there for the rest of your life. Try to choose a place that is close enough for family members and friends to visit you. Think about cost and what insurance covers, too.

Emergency services

If you need medical care right away, call 911. Tell them what the problem is. People with medical training will come to you fast. You don't have to call your doctor first.

Emergency room (ER)

An emergency room (ER), also called an emergency department (ED). It provides care when you are very sick or hurt. Go to an ER if you need healthcare right away. You don't have to call your doctor first.

Go to an ER if you have:

- Bad burns
- Broken bones
- A bad fall
- Chest pain with sweating
- Heavy bleeding
- Trouble breathing
- Very bad dizziness

Also go to an ER if you pass out, or if suddenly:

- One side of your body feels numb
- You can't see, hear, or talk
- You can't use your arms or legs

Most ERs are open 24 hours a day, every day. But if you go to the ER for something that is not an emergency, you will most likely have to wait a long time.

Hospice care

Hospice care is for people who have a terminal condition that is getting worse and cannot be cured. A doctor must order hospice care.

Hospice care can be given at home. It can also be given in an LTCF or a hospice home. Some hospitals have a special place for hospice care.

Hospice care may include:

- Medical and nursing care
- Healthcare equipment and supplies
- Help with baths and other personal care
- Help with your feelings
- Medicines to control pain and other symptoms
- Prayer and talk
- Support for your family and caregivers

Hospice care at home.

To learn more about hospice care, see page 65.

How To Choose Your Doctor

Your doctor may also be called your Primary Care Provider, or PCP for short. Your doctor knows you best and should have all your medical records.

Your doctor:

- Talks with you about your health problems and treatment options
- Works with you to make a treatment plan
- Keeps track of your symptoms and side effects
- Sends you to other doctors for tests and special care
- Collects your test results and records
- Asks about your advance care planning (see page 60)

Your doctor provides and coordinates most of your healthcare. So take the time to choose a doctor who is right for you. But choose soon—don't wait until you get sick!

1. Make a list of names

First, make a list of doctors who might work out.

You can get these names from:

- The doctor you have now (if you are moving)
- Other doctors you see
- Family members and friends
- Hospitals near you
- Your health plan
- Websites about doctors

2. Narrow down your list

Next, narrow down your list of names. Pick a few top choices.

Make sure the doctor:

- Accepts your health plan
- Uses a hospital that is in your health plan's network and that is near you
- Can arrange care when the office is closed or the doctor is busy
- Has a location and office hours that work for you
- Is licensed to practice medicine in your state
- Is taking new patients

You may also want to think about:

- How long the average wait time is
- If the doctor is a man or a woman
- What languages the doctor speaks
- If they have referral services
- If the doctor's views on health match up with your own

Special issues for seniors

Choose a doctor who knows a lot about the health needs of seniors. You can choose a geriatrician (jare-ee-uh-TRISH-un). This type of doctor is an expert in caring for seniors. Or you can choose a family practice or internal medicine doctor. These types of doctors are experts in caring for all adults.

3. Try out the doctor

Is this doctor right for you? The only way to know for sure is to set up a visit.

Before the visit

Have your records mailed or faxed to your new doctor. Or bring the records with you. You will have to sign a release of medical records form. But you have a right to get a copy of your own medical records, too. You may be charged a small fee for copying the records.

On the day of your visit

Get there early. As a new patient, you will need at least 15 minutes to fill out forms. (To learn how to get the most from your checkup, see page 42.) If you need help filling out the forms, ask the person at the front desk for help.

4. Think about the visit

After the visit, ask yourself:

- Was the office neat and clean?
- Did the staff make you feel welcome?
- How long did you need to wait? (Were you seen within 30 minutes of your scheduled appointment time?)

Did the doctor:

- Answer your questions?
- Give you enough time?
- Listen to you?
- Explain things clearly?
- Help you feel relaxed?
- Respect you?

If you answered "No" to any of these questions, you might want to choose another doctor.

Get the Most
From Your Checkups

A checkup is a visit to your doctor when you are not sick. It is usually done once a year. A checkup is also called an annual physical or annual exam.

The goal of the visit is to check your health and catch any problems early. That way, you can get treatment early.

Health history

The first time you see a new doctor, you will give your health history. You will answer questions about your health and your family's health. This history helps your doctor get to know you and make a better plan of care for you.

There may be questions about:

- Your health problems
- Health problems of your parents, grandparents, and other close family members
- How well you can manage daily needs, such as bathing
- Medicines you take
- Surgeries you have had
- Your eating, drinking, and smoking habits

You'll need to update your health history each time you see your doctor. If you have trouble filling out forms, ask if someone can help you.

Physical exam

A nurse or doctor will check your height and weight. He or she will also take your temperature, pulse (heartbeats per minute), and blood pressure (the force of blood against your artery walls). For some exams you will need to undress and put on a paper gown.

Your doctor may also:

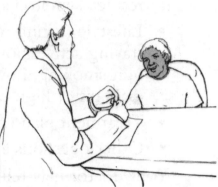

Tell the doctor about your health.

- Feel for lumps on your body
- Listen to your heart, lungs, and belly
- Look at your skin
- Look in your eyes, ears, nose, and mouth
- Push on your belly and other places to see if anything hurts
- Test your reflexes
- Watch you get out of a chair and walk
- Check your memory

If you are a **woman**, your doctor may also:

- Feel your breasts for lumps. This is called a breast exam.
- Feel your lower belly and inside your vagina. This is called a pelvic exam.
- Reach into your vagina to collect cells from your cervix. This is called a Pap smear. The cells will be sent to a lab to check for cervical cancer.

If you are a **man**, your doctor may also:

- Reach into your rectum to check the size of your prostate and feel for lumps. This is called a prostate exam.

Talking with your doctor

At the checkup, you and your doctor may talk about these things:

- Health problems (test results, symptoms)
- Lifestyle (eating well, staying active, how to quit smoking, how to manage your chronic illnesses, like diabetes or high blood pressure)
- Treatment plan (how well it works, side effects)
- Other questions and concerns

Your doctor may tell you to do these things:

- Change your treatment plan
- Get tests or vaccines
- Go to another doctor for an exam

What you can do

Before the visit:

Get informed. Learn as much as you can about your health problems and treatments.

Keep track of your health. Write down your symptoms and side effects.

Make a list of medicines.

Make a list of medicines you take. Include prescription and over-the-counter drugs. Also include vitamins and herbs. (You can use the chart on page 55.)

Get the Most From Your Checkups

Make a list of questions. Put the most important ones at the top of your list. Feel free to ask any question, even if it seems silly or embarrassing.

During the visit:

Ask questions. And keep asking until you understand. For instance, say, "Let me make sure I have this right …"

Write down your questions.

Bring a friend or family member. This person can help you listen or take notes. But do the talking yourself, if you can.

Bring your notes. Tell your doctor about your symptoms, side effects, and medicines.

Take notes. After a visit, it can be hard to recall what your doctor said. So write down key facts, such as your blood pressure. Or use a recorder.

Wear your hearing aid, glasses, and dentures. Take your cane or walker if you use one. They will help you communicate better. Plus, your doctor can see how well these items work for you.

Get Needed Tests and Vaccines

You need certain tests and vaccines to help you stay well. Some are routine. Others are done only if you may have a health problem. Ask your doctor which tests and vaccines (shots) are right for you. Sometimes, after a certain age, or if you are too sick, some tests may not be needed.

Tests you may need

Tests are used to check for health problems. Here are some tests you may need:

Blood sugar test. This checks how much sugar is in your blood. Too much sugar in the blood can be a sign of diabetes.

Cholesterol test. This checks how much cholesterol is in your blood. Some types of cholesterol can block your arteries.

Hearing test. This checks how well you can hear. You may wear headphones and listen for sounds during the test.

Vision test. This checks how well your eyes work. You may follow a light with your eyes during the test. You may also be asked to read some letters or numbers.

Stool test. This checks for blood in a sample of your stool (feces), which can be a sign of early colon cancer.

Mammogram. This checks for breast cancer at an early stage. An x-ray takes a picture of the inside of your breasts.

Sigmoidoscopy (sig-moy-DOS-kuh-pee). This lets the doctor look for cancer inside the lower part of your large intestine. The doctor puts a small, lighted tube into your rectum. The doctor may also remove any growths (polyps).

Colonoscopy (co-luh-NOS-kuh-pee). This lets the doctor look for cancer inside your whole large intestine. The doctor puts a small, lighted tube into your rectum. The doctor may also remove any growths (polyps).

Get ready for the test

Ask your doctor:

- Where to get the test done. Some tests can be done at your doctor's office. Others must be done at a hospital or test center.
- What to expect during the test. For instance, find out if it will hurt or if there are risks.
- What you should do to get ready. For instance, find out if you need to fast (not eat or drink) for a certain amount of time.

Vaccines (shots) you may need

Vaccines help protect you from diseases that can make you sick, or even kill you. Some vaccines must be given by injection (shot). Others can be breathed in through the nose.

Get Needed Tests and Vaccines

This chart shows common vaccines for seniors. It tells how often to get them. Check the box and put in the date when you get each shot.

Done/ Date	What vaccine	How often	Remember
	Flu	Every year	Get it by the middle of November.
	Pneumonia	Once in your life after 65	There are 2 types of pneumonia vaccine. You need one of each type. You may also need a second dose.
	Tetanus and Diphtheria	Every 10 years	Also get it if you have a deep or dirty cut.
	Whooping Cough	Once as an adult	It comes as part of certain tetanus and diphtheria vaccines.
	Shingles	Once in your life after 60	Get it even if you've never had chicken pox.

Get ready for the vaccine

Ask your doctor:

- What vaccines you need. If you have certain health problems, such as diabetes or no spleen, there are other vaccines you may need.

- Where to get the vaccine. You may be able to get it at your doctor's office or the health department. Some pharmacies, stores, and other places give vaccines.

- How the vaccine will affect you. Unless you have an allergy to a vaccine, it will not make you sick. But you may have a sore arm or a low fever after you get a shot. Taking acetaminophen (Tylenol) may help.

Keep a record

Ask for a copy of your test results. Write down the vaccines you get. Keep them in a safe place.

Take Charge of Your Medicines

When you take charge of your medicines, you know which medicines you take. You take these medicines the way you were told to take them. This lets you get the most from your treatment.

Know the different types of medicine

Brand-name and generic drugs

Most medicines have both a brand-name form and a generic form. For example, Motrin is a brand-name drug, and ibuprofen is the generic form of that same drug.

Generics often cost less than brand-name drugs. But they work just as well. The law says these drugs must have the same amount of the active part as the brand-name drug does. Some medicines do not have a generic form.

Prescription drugs

Your doctor must prescribe these medicines. The doctor may write the prescription on a piece of paper and give it to you. Or the doctor may call the pharmacy or send the prescription to the pharmacy by computer.

Prescription for medicine

It is best to get all your prescription drugs from the same pharmacy. That way, the pharmacist will know if a new medicine could cause a problem, such as a drug allergy or drug interaction.

Before you leave the pharmacy, make sure you know how to take the medicine. If you're not sure, ask the pharmacist before you leave.

Getting refills

Sometimes you can buy more of a prescription drug without seeing the doctor. This is called a refill. You may be able to get automatic refills.

The label will say how many refills you can get. If you aren't sure, ask the pharmacist. Call your doctor or pharmacy before you run out of refills. Check with your health insurance company. You may be able to get your refills by mail. Ask if they provide online ordering.

Choosing your pharmacy

- Choose a pharmacy that accepts your health plan.
- Compare prices, and ask about senior discounts.
- Make sure the location and hours work for you. Or choose a pharmacy that has home delivery.
- Use the same pharmacy for all your prescriptions. That way, they can keep track of your drug allergies and interactions.

Your pharmacy can help

Ask if staff will:

- Call to remind you when you need refills
- Call you when refills are ready
- Fill weekly pillboxes for you
- Print the label in your language
- Put different medicines in different-colored bottles
- Use caps that are easy to open
- Use large bottles that are easy to hold
- Use large print on labels

Over-the-counter (OTC) drugs

You can buy these drugs without a prescription. Tell your doctor about all the OTC drugs you take. Some OTCs don't mix well with prescription drugs. They can change how your prescription drugs work. Talk to your doctor before you take any new OTCs.

OTC drugs include:

- Cold medicines
- Antacids
- Herbal remedies
- Laxatives
- Pain medicines
- Sleep aids
- Vitamins and minerals

Special OTC dosing for seniors

You may not need to take as much as a younger adult takes. Ask your doctor or pharmacist how much you should take. Ask if they are safe for you.

Keep track of problems you may have with your medicine

Drug allergies

Some people have a drug allergy. If they take a medicine they are allergic to, they may get very sick or even die.

If you have a drug allergy:

- Tell your doctor about it. Make sure it is in your chart.
- Tell your pharmacist. Make sure it goes in your record.
- Before you start taking a new medicine, find out if it contains anything that you are allergic to. Ask your doctor or pharmacist if you are not sure.

If you have an allergic reaction:

- Your lips, tongue, and face may swell.
- You may get a rash. It may or may not itch.
- You may have trouble breathing.

If you think you may be having an allergic reaction, get medical help right away.

An allergic reaction
to a medicine can be
an emergency.
Stop taking the medicine.
Call 911, or go to the
nearest ER if you have
trouble breathing.

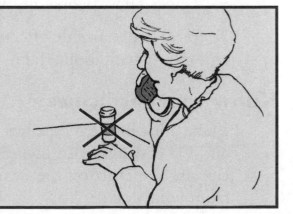

Take Charge of Your Medicines

Drug interactions

Some drugs affect the way other drugs work. Some foods and drinks also affect the way drugs work. These changes are called drug interactions.

That's why it's important to tell your doctor about all the medicines you take. Include prescription and OTC drugs. Also include vitamins and herbs. Ask if you should avoid certain foods and drinks.

Side effects

Side effects are ways that a medicine affects your body besides treating your illness. For example, some drugs may make you feel dizzy or sick to your stomach.

Ask the pharmacist about side effects.

When you start a new medicine, ask your doctor what side effects you may have. Read the label too. Keep in mind that medicines affect people in different ways.

Keep track of any side effects you have. Tell your doctor and pharmacist about them.

Know your medicines

Make a list of the medicines you take. Include prescription and OTC drugs. Also include vitamins and herbs. You can use the chart on the next page. Don't rely on a list from your doctor. You may have medicines given to you by other doctors. List them all. List any changes to your medicines.

Take Charge of Your Medicines

List of Medicines

Prescription medicines

Medicine	Why taken	Color	How much	When
(Example) Cipro 250 mg	To treat my urinary tract infection	Red	1 capsule 4 times a day	9 am 1 pm 5 pm 9 pm

Over-the-counter medicines

(check here if you are using any of these)

❑ Laxatives

❑ Antacids

❑ Vitamins

❑ Cold medicine

❑ Cough medicine

❑ Aspirin/ pain reliever

❑ Sleeping pills

❑ Allergy

❑ Herbal remedies

Other (names)

❑ _____

❑ _____

❑ _____

❑ _____

Ask about your medicines

Before you start taking a medicine, make sure you know how to take it. Make sure you know why you are taking it.

Ask your doctor or pharmacist:

- What is the name of the medicine?
- Does it come in a generic form?
- Why should I take it?
- When should I take it?
- How long should I take it?
- Will my dose change due to my age?
- How will I know it's working?

Is it generic?

Yes, it is.

- What are the side effects?
- What should I do if I forget to take a dose?
- Are there any foods I should not eat while taking it?
- Are there other medicines or vitamins I should not take while taking it?
- Can I drive while taking it?
- How should I store this medicine?
- How can I learn more about it?

Be safe with your medicines

Take medicines safely

1. Wash your hands. That way, you won't make yourself sick.

2. Read the label. Make sure it's for you. If you need to, turn on a light or use a magnifying glass to help you see.

3. Look at the medicine. Is it the right color and shape?

4. Take your medicine exactly as you were told to take it. Follow the directions.

5. Sit or stand. Don't lie down.

6. If you have trouble swallowing, ask your doctor what to do. Don't crush, break, or open pills unless your doctor or pharmacist says it's OK.

7. Measure liquids the right way. Ask your pharmacist what to use to measure how much you take.

Store medicines safely

• Always keep your medicine in the container that it came in. (But it's OK to put your dose for the day in your weekly pillbox.)

• Keep your medicine away from heat and bright light.

• Keep your medicine out of sight and away from where children and pets can get to it.

• Store it in a cool, dry place. Do not store it in your bathroom.

Be safe when you throw away drugs and supplies

• Check the dates every 6 months. Get rid of medicine that is out-of-date.

• Bring your old medicine to your pharmacy. Don't just flush it.

• Use a special container for used needles and syringes. Ask your pharmacist for one.

• Never give your medicine away or take someone else's medicine.

Take your medicines the right way

Keep track of your medicines.

- Keep each medicine in the container it came in.
- Make a weekly dosing chart. Cross out each dose after you take it.
- Take each medicine at the same time each day.
- Use an alarm clock or timer to remind you to take your medicines.
- Use a weekly pillbox.

Here's an example of a dosing chart:

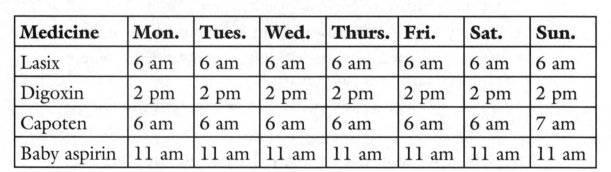

Medicine	Mon.	Tues.	Wed.	Thurs.	Fri.	Sat.	Sun.
Lasix	6 am	6 am	6 am	6 am	6 am	6 am	6 am
Digoxin	2 pm	2 pm	2 pm	2 pm	2 pm	2 pm	2 pm
Capoten	6 am	6 am	6 am	6 am	6 am	6 am	7 am
Baby aspirin	11 am	11 am	11 am	11 am	11 am	11 am	11 am

If you miss a dose

Ask your doctor what to do.

Your doctor may tell you to:

- Skip the dose and take the next one, OR
- Take 2 doses the next time, OR
- Take the dose right away.

Tell your doctor if you are often forgetting to take your medicine.

Take Charge of Your Medicines

Talk with your doctor before you stop taking a medicine

Keep taking your medicine:

- **If you feel better.** That might be because the medicine is working.

- **If you don't feel better.** Give the medicine more time. Some medicines take weeks to start working. Some may be working even if you can't tell.

- **If you think you have side effects.** Ask your doctor how to handle or reduce the side effects. Or ask about other medicines you could take instead.

- **If your doctor tells you to stop a medicine**, also tell your pharmacy so they do not refill it. Be sure to tell your other doctors, too.

- Tell your doctor if you are worried about being able to pay for your medicine.

When you travel

- Bring more medicine than you think you will need.
- Keep your medicines separate. Don't mix them together in one medicine bottle.
- Never leave your medicine in a car.
- When you fly, keep your medicine with you in your carry-on bag.

How to Make
Your Wishes Known

Every adult should have an advance directive. You do not need to be old or sick to fill one out. An advance directive tells what healthcare you want if you become too ill to say what care you want. A serious accident or illness can happen at any time. It is best to make your wishes for end-of-life care known while you are well.

Think about your choices

Making end-of-life choices is not simple. Think carefully, and talk to your doctor if you are not sure what a choice may mean for you.

Some of these choices are:

- If you cannot eat, do you want to be fed through a tube?
- If your heart or breathing stops, do you want someone to push on your chest and breathe into your mouth to rescue you?
- Do you want a machine to help you breathe if you cannot breathe on your own?
- Would you change any of your choices if you could not move or take care of yourself?
- Would you change any of your choices if you were in a coma (not awake and unable to wake up for an extended time)? Or if you had bad memory loss?
- Would you be OK if you had to move to a nursing home?

Talk with your family members, friends, and doctor

Tell them clearly what you want and why. Let them know if you change your mind about any of your choices. That way, they won't be surprised.

Put your choices in writing

Write down your choices on a legal form. Or go online to prepareforyourcare.org to fill out your wishes. Your doctor and hospital care teams have to honor your end-of-life choices if you have filled out a legal form. These choices are followed if you are too ill to talk.

There are 2 parts of an advance directive:

- **Living will.** This form lets you say what healthcare you want or don't want when you are too ill to talk.

- **Durable power of attorney for healthcare.** This form lets you name someone you trust to make healthcare choices for you when you are too ill to talk. This person is called your healthcare agent, or healthcare proxy. Make sure your healthcare agent wants

Have a legal paper that tells your choices when you cannot speak for yourself.

to have this role. And make sure they know clearly what you want—and what you don't want.

You can use one or both of these forms. Some states combine them.

How to Make Your Wishes Known

Many states have passed laws to allow one form to be followed as "doctor's orders." This form is called a POLST (Physician Orders for Life-Sustaining Treatment). Many states have laws about this now. This form will allow emergency workers in the ambulance to be able to get these doctor's orders about what to do or not do when called. A signed POLST form is the best way to make sure that your "wishes" related to end-of-life care are followed. It provides doctor's orders for all healthcare workers.

Sign and date these forms

In order for these forms to be legal, you must sign and date them. A person who saw you sign must also sign them. This person is called a witness. You may also need to have this form signed by a person called a Notary Public.

Where to get these forms

Here are some places to get these forms:

- Bookstore
- Doctor's office
- Senior center
- Hospital
- Nursing home
- Library
- Online (visit prepareforyourcare.org or www.iha4health. org/our-services/advance-directive)

Put your forms in a safe place. Check off each box when you have done that step.

- ❑ Tell your family members and friends where to find your legal forms. Or give them a copy.
- ❑ Give a copy to your doctor.
- ❑ Bring a copy to the hospital, surgery center, or ER.
- ❑ If you call 911, have someone get your forms.

❑ Carry a copy of your durable power of attorney for healthcare in your purse or wallet.

❑ Give a copy to your faith community leader, in case of an emergency.

Talk to your family about your choices.

Get support

It can be hard to decide what you want for end-of-life care. It can also be hard to make sense of legal forms. It's better to think about and make these decisions ahead of time.

Here are some places to get support:

• Family members and friends
• Office that gives services to seniors, including legal aid agencies
• Your faith community
• Senior center
• Your doctor

Palliative Care

Palliative (PALLY-uh-tiv) care is special medical care for people with serious illnesses. It helps you feel better and feel less stress. The goal is better quality of life for you and your family.

Palliative care is given by a special team. This includes doctors, nurses and social workers. They work with your other doctors to provide an extra layer of support. You can have palliative care at any age and stage of your illness. You can also get palliative care at the same time as treatment meant to cure you.

Palliative care treats things like cancer, heart disease, lung disease, kidney disease, Alzheimer's and many more.

Palliative care helps with:

- Pain and symptom control

- Communication and decision-making

- Coordination

- Emotional support

- Family/caregiver support

Palliative care treats things like pain, shortness of breath, being very tired, trouble having a BM, upset stomach, loss of appetite, trouble falling asleep, and depression.

It helps you gain the strength to carry on with daily life. It helps you to be able to handle your treatments. And it helps you to better understand your choices.

You can expect the best possible quality of life.

Hospice

Hospice care is usually a choice if you have a terminal health condition. You must be considered gravely ill and within 6 months of death to be eligible for most hospice programs. Your doctor must order hospice care, and your insurance company must approve it. Once approved, hospice care is provided by a team of hospice professionals.

Hospice programs provide:

- Care given in your home or a nursing home
- Care is provided by a family caregiver, as well as a visiting hospice nurse
- Comfort rather than aggressive disease reduction
- Emotional support for you and your family
- Help in dealing with the real issues of dying

Most programs concentrate on your comfort. By not using therapies that just keep you alive longer, hospice patients can focus on getting the most out of the time they have left, without some of the negative side effects. Most hospice patients can get to a level of comfort that lets them focus on the emotional and practical issues of dying.

Hospice programs are covered by Medicare. Palliative and hospice programs do serve different goals. Talk to your doctor about the best service for you.

How to Handle Normal Changes

3

As you get older, your body goes through many changes. It's important to know what is normal and when you should talk to your doctor. The good news is that some of these changes can be controlled through lifestyle changes, medicines, and other treatments.

Notes

_____

_____

_____

_____

_____

_____

_____

_____

_____

_____

_____

Deciding Where to Live

You may need to think about where you will live during your senior years. As you grow older your needs will change. You may need more help with things you do every day.

You may need more medical care. It may get hard to do things that you need to do around your home. These may include

- Shop for groceries
- Drive at night, a long way, or through heavy traffic
- Clean your house
- Do laundry
- Pay your bills

You may need help with your normal daily life. These are called activities of daily living (ADLs). Here are some ADLs you do each day:

- Bathe
- Groom
- Eat
- Dress
- Use the toilet

You may need help taking care of your pets.

Think about your choices for where you should live before you need to change. That way you will have more control over your choice. Take time to talk to people. Visit your housing choices. Make your decision. Move when you are in good health. This will give you time to know your new community and make new

Deciding Where to Live

friends. When you find the right place for you to live, it will help you have a healthy and happy life.

Here are some choices to think about for where you should live:

Aging in place means you will stay in your own home. Here are some reasons to choose this:

- You know your neighbors, and your community is safe
- You have friends
- You can afford to stay there
- You do not need a lot of physical or medical care
- You have services that you can use to help with housekeeping, yard work or trips to the doctor's office
- You have family nearby
- Your home does not have a lot of steps
- The doorways are wide enough for wheelchairs
- Some changes, like grab bars, railings, or an emergency call system, have been added to your home.

Accessory dwelling units are backyard apartments, garages, or basement homes which have been added to a home. Here are some reasons to choose this:

- Caregiver or family can live in the house on the same property
- You do not need a lot of physical or medical care
- You have services that you can hire to help with housekeeping, transportation, or home delivery
- You already have friends
- You have activities that you can do
- You have an emergency call system

Deciding Where to Live

Independent living is a community of homes for seniors. It may have these services, which you pay for:

- Housekeeping services
- Meals served like in a restaurant
- Transportation
- Social and exercise activities

Only choose independent living if you do not need help with ADLs. There is no help for medical care, medicines, or supervision. An emergency call system should be in place.

Assisted living is a good choice if you need help with ADLs. You may need help with medicines. It may be a room, an apartment, or a condo. Most places have group eating and activities. This kind of home does not have round-the-clock medical care or supervision.

Nursing home. You can get care and help with ADLs 24 hours a day. Choose this if you need a high level of medical care. This is the most costly type of senior housing.

Continuing care community has all levels of care in one location: independent, assisted, and dependent (nursing home). You can move from one level to another in the same facility. A senior can stay in one area as their housing needs change over time. It often means that spouses can stay very close to each other, even if one spouse needs different housing.

Affordable housing for low-income people can be found in most communities. This may be a room, an apartment, rental help, or help to live in your own home. There can be long wait lists for this. Put your name in well before you may need it.

Get ready for a change. Most people after age 65 need to look for senior housing. Accept that you may need to make a change.

Deciding Where to Live

Keep an open mind. Try not to say things like, "I'll never live in a place like that." Know that you will need to make new friends. Work at making the best choice for yourself.

Before you begin to look for housing, make a list of what you need now. You might add something that you know about your needs changing as you continue to grow older.

Here are some ideas to help with your list:

Meals <u>getting harder to shop for groceries and cook meals</u>

Wheelchair / walker accessible _____

Help with bathing_____

Help with taking medicine_____

Help with walking_____

Driving_____

Medical_____

Help with activities of daily living_____

Help with housekeeping _____

Hobbies and things you like to do _____

Friends and family_____

Religion or faith _____

Caring for a pet_____

Safety _____

Your budget_____

_____

Talk with others about senior housing and senior services in your community. Talk with your doctor, social worker, and friends. Use your list to ask questions.

Look for housing. Visit senior housing in your community. Visit more than once. Visit at different times of the day. Will it be easy to have friends? It is OK to use your gut feelings. You will need to make very sure that the level of care you

need will be met. You know exactly what services come with the housing. Make sure that you understand what your contract says. And finally, know what the exact cost will be.

Getting help. You may need help having a family planning meeting. You may need help finding senior housing that you can afford. Or, you may need help looking at and choosing senior housing. Your community will have help for you.

Here are some other places to get help:

- Local newspapers
- Booklets on senior housing
- Search online
- Ask at the place you get your medical care
- Check with government agencies like your local Area Agency on Aging, Department of Elder Affairs or HUD, the U.S. Department of Housing and Urban Development, social worker (ask your doctor), or your local Department on Aging.

Vision Changes

Your vision changes as you get older. You may get more farsighted. That means you have trouble seeing things that are close to you. When you read, the print may look blurry.

You may also get eyestrain more easily. That means your eyes get red and sore. This can happen when you look at things up close for a long time.

Farsighted

- Choose books and magazines with large print.
- Use a magnifying glass to read.
- Wear the right glasses.
- When you type on a computer, use a large type size (14 point or larger).
- Use good lighting.

Wear eyeglasses, and use light when reading.

Eyestrain

Be sure to blink. Blinking keeps your eyes moist.

Take breaks. When you look at things up close, take a break every 20 minutes. Look at something in the distance. This lets your eyes rest.

Use plenty of light. But avoid glare.

Keep eyes moist. Ask your doctor about using drops.

Take care of your eyes

Don't smoke. Smoking can make you more likely to get eye problems.

Eat right. Some foods can protect you from eye problems. Choose dark leafy greens, such as spinach. Also eat items high in omega-3 fatty acids, such as salmon.

Know your family history. Many eye problems can be passed down.

Protect your eyes from sunlight. Sunlight can cause eye problems. When you go outside, wear a hat with a wide brim. Wear sunglasses that block ultraviolet (UV) light.

See the doctor. Get your eyes checked each year. Also see your eye doctor if you have any symptoms of eye problems.

Stay at a healthy weight. Being overweight raises your risk of diabetes, which can cause eye problems.

Watch out for eye problems

As you get older, you are more likely to have eye problems. Watch out for these problems so you can get treatment early.

Cataracts

A cataract happens when the lens in your eye is cloudy. Things may look blurred. The cataract may get worse over time.

If a cataract harms your sight, you can get surgery. An eye doctor will take out your cloudy lens and put in a new one.

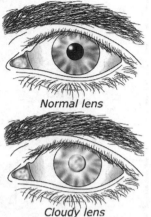

Normal lens

Cloudy lens

Glaucoma

Glaucoma happens when fluid builds up inside your eye. Your eye may be red and very painful. Or you may have no symptoms.

If you have glaucoma, get treatment right away. Otherwise, you may go blind. Get screened once a year.

Glaucoma is treated with pills and eyedrops. In some cases, you may need surgery.

Macular degeneration

Macular degeneration happens when a spot inside your eye stops working. This is the spot that helps you see small details. Your sight may fade or get blurry. You may not be able to see things straight on or in the center of your vision. But there is no pain.

Macular degeneration is the leading cause of vision loss in seniors. It can often be treated if your doctor finds it early.

Get help right away

Call your eye doctor right away if you have:

- Bad eye pain
- Fluid coming from your eye
- Red or swollen and painful eyes
- See double
- See flashes of light
- See rings around lights
- Suddenly can't see
- Suddenly have blurred vision

Hearing Changes

Your hearing changes as you get older. About 1 in 3 people between ages 65 and 74 has hearing loss. About 1 in 2 people older than 74 has hearing loss. This can make you feel lonely and isolated.

You may have trouble hearing, especially when there is background noise. Answer these questions. If you answer "yes" to 3 or more, ask your doctor to test your hearing.

Do you have a problem hearing people on the phone?	❑ Yes	❑ No
Do you have trouble hearing when there is noise in the background?	❑ Yes	❑ No
Is it hard for you to follow a conversation when people talk at the same time?	❑ Yes	❑ No
Do you have to try hard to understand a conversation?	❑ Yes	❑ No
Does it seem like people mumble when they talk to you?	❑ Yes	❑ No
Do you often misunderstand what others are saying?	❑ Yes	❑ No
Do you often ask people to repeat things?	❑ Yes	❑ No
Do people complain that you turn the TV volume up too high?	❑ Yes	❑ No

Talk with your doctor

If you are concerned about changes in hearing, talk with your doctor. Ask about treatments and if you should see an expert. Ask if you should take a hearing test.

Keep your ears clean

Earwax can make it harder to hear. Ask your doctor to check your ears for earwax. Ask about the best way to clean your ears.

Use your eyes

Good eyes can help a little if you have poor hearing. Keep your glasses up-to-date, and wear them. Use good lighting.

Have a doctor check your ears for too much earwax.

Limit background noise

Background noise can make it harder to hear.

- Find a quiet place to talk.
- Turn off the TV and radio.
- When you go out to eat, ask for a quiet table.

Let technology work for you

- If you get a hearing aid, learn how to use it, and wear it. If you can't afford a hearing aid, talk to your doctor about other options.
- Set your cell phone to vibrate when it rings.
- Turn up the volume on your phone.
- Use email and text messages.

- When you watch TV, turn on captions.
- When you watch videos, turn on subtitles in your language.

Tell people

You have the right to hear. So tell friends, family members, and healthcare providers when you have trouble hearing.

Wear your hearing aid.

Ask them to:

- Repeat things
- Speak louder
- Face you, so you can see their mouth move
- Sit on your "good" side
- Write down what they want to say

A note on tinnitus

If you have tinnitus (tin-NIGH-tuss), you hear noise all the time. You may hear it in one or both ears. The noise may sound like a hiss, roar, bell, or chirp. It can make it hard to hear or sleep.

If you have ringing in your ears, talk to your doctor. Ask about treatments and if you should see an expert.

Get help right away

Call your doctor right away if:

- Fluid comes out of your ear
- You are dizzy and don't know why
- You have sudden hearing loss in one or both ears
- Your hearing aid does not work
- You have pain in your ear
- You have ringing in your ear

Taste and Smell Changes

It is common for your senses of taste and smell to change as you get older. They fade over time. Sometimes problems with your teeth or dentures can change your taste and smell.

Talk with your doctor

If you are concerned about these changes, talk with your doctor. Ask if you are taking any medicines that affect your taste and smell. Ask your dentist to check your teeth or dentures. If you smoke, ask your doctor to help you quit. Smoking can dull these senses.

Make food fun—boost your other senses

- **Boost color.** Try red beets, green chard, and yellow peppers.
- **Boost flavor.** Try chilies, garlic, herbs, and lemon. Don't use extra salt unless your doctor says it's OK.
- **Boost texture.** Try foods that are creamy, crunchy, and chewy.
- **Boost variety.** Try foods that you've never had before.

Get enough to eat

Changes in taste and smell can make it hard to enjoy eating. If chewing is hard with dentures, talk to your dentist. But for the sake of your health, make sure to eat plenty of healthy food (see page 126). Smoothies are a good way to get all the nutrition you need. You can make them with fruit, vegetables, nut butters, or milk. If you find yourself losing weight, tell your doctor.

Keep food safe

Your nose may no longer tell you when food has gone bad. So write the date on any food that could spoil. Throw it out after 4 days.

Ask your friends and family for help

Ask them to tell you about smells that you may not notice. They can tell you if you have body odor or wear too much perfume. They can tell you if you have a gas leak in your home.

Memory Changes

Your memory changes as you get older. It may get worse over time. You may misplace your keys or glasses. You may forget to take your medicine or water the plants. These things are normal. But sometimes these changes are more than they should be. There are different kinds of memory loss.

Talk with your doctor

If you are concerned about memory changes, talk with your doctor. Memory loss can be caused by many things:

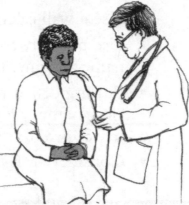

Talk to your doctor about being forgetful.

- Some medicines
- Heart disease
- Brain diseases such as Alzheimer's

Ask about treatments. (To learn more about Alzheimer's disease, see page 104.)

Prevent memory loss

- Keep active, and stay connected to family and friends.
- Get plenty of sleep, healthy food, and fluid (see page 125).
- Limit alcohol (see page 146).
- Stay active (see page 133).
- Call or visit family and friends.
- Take your medicine the right way, every time (see page 58).

How to handle memory loss

- Make lists of things to do.
- Put things back in the same place each time.
- Set timers and alarms.
- Try to think about just one thing at a time.
- Use a daily pillbox.
- Use a wall calendar.
- Use memory tricks. For instance, if you meet someone named Penny, link Penny's name to the coin.
- Put important phone numbers in your cell phone with clear names. For instance, WellDrug Pharmacy, tel. 333-3333, Pharmacist: John.
- Consider an ID or "safe return" bracelet.

Get help right away

Call your doctor right away if:

- Someone you know gets lost or can't remember where they live
- You have a sudden loss of memory, or it gets worse

Sleep Changes

Your sleeping habits change as you get older. You may:

- Feel tired during the day
- Have trouble falling asleep
- Not sleep deeply
- Wake often because of pain or the need to urinate

Talk with your doctor

If you are concerned about sleeping changes, talk with your doctor. Ask about treatments.

Make your bedroom a sleep zone

Cover the windows with dark blinds or drapes, and keep the room cool and dark. Use the bed only for sleep and sex. Do not read or watch TV in bed.

Follow good sleeping habits

During the day:

- Limit alcohol and caffeine (see page 146).

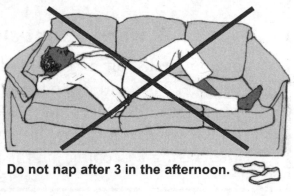

- Limit naps to 30 minutes before 3 in the afternoon.

Do not nap after 3 in the afternoon.

- Stay active before 3 in the afternoon.
- Stop drinking 4 hours before bed. That way, you won't wake up to go to the bathroom as often.

At night:

- Give yourself at least 20 minutes to fall asleep. If you can't sleep, get up and read, or watch TV. Go back to bed when you feel sleepy.

- Have a set time to go to sleep and to wake up.

- Take a bath or read a book before bedtime to make you sleepy.

- Try not to think about things that worry you.

A word about sleeping pills

Sleeping pills can make it harder to keep your balance. They can make you more likely to fall if you get up at night. Sleeping pills can also make you feel hung over the next day. It may not be safe to drive after taking a sleeping pill the night before.

Skin Changes

Your skin changes as you get older. It may get thinner, drier, and less stretchy. It may get looser and more wrinkled. Your skin may bruise more easily and take longer to heal. It may get more spots and moles. You are also more likely to get skin cancer, especially if you have fair skin.

Check for signs of cancer

Early treatment could save your life. So check your skin once every few months for signs of cancer. Or have a partner check it.

Tell your doctor if you find:

- Brown or black spot that changes in color or size
- Brown or black spot that is bigger than a pencil eraser
- Rough or bumpy red area that is bigger than the head of a match
- Skin that is red, itchy, cracked, or bleeding
- Sore that takes more than 2 weeks to heal

Protect your skin from sun damage

The sun can cause wrinkles and skin cancer. So avoid going outside when the sun is strong. When you do go outside, wear:

- A hat with a wide brim

Wear a wide-brim hat to shade your face.

- Long sleeves and pants. Choose lightweight ones in hot weather.
- Sunblock that blocks UVA and UVB rays. The higher the SPF (Sun Protection Factor), the better.
- Sunglasses that block UVA and UVB rays

Keep skin soft and smooth

This helps protect your skin from tears and sores.

- Bathe every few days in warm (not hot) water.
- Choose soaps that are gentle to your skin.
- Choose creams and lip balms with petroleum jelly. You can also use natural oils like coconut oil.
- Drink plenty of fluid.
- If you smoke, quit.
- Rinse off after you swim in a pool.
- Use a humidifier if the air in your home is dry.

Thinking about surgery?

There is surgery to smooth out your skin. Before you get it, ask about risks, costs, and how long it works. Medicare will pay for surgery only if the skin around your eyes blocks your sight so much that you can't drive safely.

Foot Changes

Your feet change with age. As you get older:

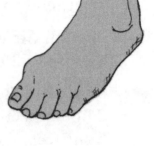

- Arthritis may make your feet stiff and painful.
- You may have less blood flow to your feet.
- Some medicines may make your legs and feet swell.
- The fat pads on your feet may get thinner.
- Your feet may get longer and wider.
- The skin on your feet may be dry.
- Your toenails may get thicker. They may get fungus and break more often.

Choose the right shoes

Buy new fitness shoes each year. Their padding wears out.

Choose shoes you can use. If you have trouble lacing your shoes, look for Velcro. If you have trouble bending down, get shoes you can slip on. But lace-up shoes are safer.

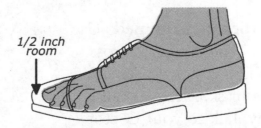

1/2 inch room

Cushion your feet. Choose shoes with good padding. Or buy padded inserts.

Make sure your shoes fit well. There should be ½ inch between your longest toe and the end of the shoe. Try on both shoes before you buy them. Buy shoes late in the day. Feet tend to swell during the day.

Switch off what shoes you wear. Try not to wear the same pair 2 days in a row.

Wear low heels. They should be less than 1½ inches high. Higher heels put too much weight on the front part of your feet. You also have more chance of falling or twisting your ankle.

Groom your feet

Keep your feet clean. Dry them well—even between your toes. This helps prevent fungus.

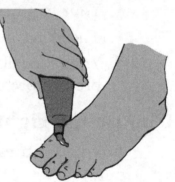

Use cream on your feet.

Keep your skin soft and smooth. Soak your feet in warm, not hot, water. This will soften corns and calluses—layers of dead skin. Gently smooth your skin with a pumice stone. Put cream on your feet at night.

Keep your toenails trimmed. Use nail clippers. Trim straight across. File down sharp edges. Make sure not to cut your skin. If you can't do this safely, talk to your doctor or visit a podiatrist (foot doctor).

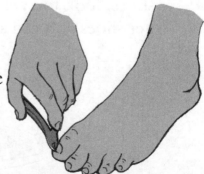

Trim toenails straight across.

Wear clean socks each day. Use cotton socks if your feet sweat. If you wear shoes without socks, you might get blisters.

Improve blood flow to your feet

- Avoid socks that squeeze your legs (unless your doctor tells you to wear them).
- Get up and move around each hour. This will boost blood flow in your legs and feet.
- Try not to cross your legs.

Watch out for foot problems

Tell your doctor if you find corns, fungus, ingrown toenails, or warts. Ask about treatments and if you should see an expert.

If you have diabetes

Diabetes can lower blood flow to your feet or decrease feeling in them. That makes it harder to know when you get a cut. So always wear shoes.

Diabetes also makes it harder for cuts to heal. So check your feet each day. Tell your doctor about any cuts, cracks, red marks, or sores.

Hard Stools (Constipation)

As you get older, you are more likely to get hard stools. That's because your bowels move slower over time.

Your stools may be dry, hard, and small. You may also need to strain in order to move your bowels.

Talk with your doctor

If you are concerned about hard stools, talk with your doctor. Ask about treatments.

Keep your bowels regular

- Some people need more fiber. Ask your doctor about your needs. In general, women over 50 should eat 21 grams of fiber each day. Men over 50 should eat 30 grams of fiber a day. You can get it from the food you eat (see page 126). You can also get it from bran or supplements.
- Drink plenty of fluids (if your doctor says it's OK).
- Have a bowel movement when you feel the urge—don't wait.
- Stay active (see page 133).
- Take a stool softener. This is a pill. Do not use it for more than 3 days unless your doctor says it's OK.
- Talk to your doctor if you do not have regular bowel movements. Ask if your medicines are affecting your bowel movements.
- When you wake up, drink warm or hot fluids. Make sure to eat breakfast.

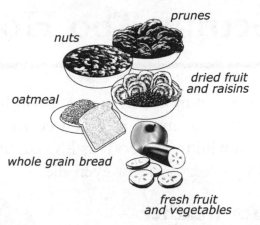

nuts

prunes

dried fruit and raisins

oatmeal

whole grain bread

fresh fruit and vegetables

Here are some good sources of fiber.

Train your bowels

You may be able to train your bowels to move on schedule.

Follow these steps each day:

- Have breakfast.
- Sit on the toilet for 15 minutes. Relax—don't strain.
- If your bowels don't move, try again 20 minutes after your next meal.

Get help right away

Call your doctor right away if:

- There is blood in your stool
- You get bad stomach pains
- You have not had a bowel movement in more than 3 days, and you have bad pain
- You throw up
- Your stomach is very hard

Getting Too Hot

As you get older, you are more likely to get too hot. That's because you don't sweat as much as you used to. Plus, you may not feel thirsty, even when your body is low on fluids. If you get too hot, you could get very sick, or even die.

Stay cool in hot weather

Avoid caffeine and alcohol. They make you pass urine more often. That can make your body low on fluids.

Dress for the weather. Choose loose, lightweight cotton fabric that lets your skin breathe.

Eat cool foods. Salads are a good choice.

Drink water to stay cool in hot weather.

Have plenty of cold drinks (if your doctor says it's OK). Remember, your body may need more fluid, even if you don't feel thirsty.

Shower or bathe in cool water. Take more than one per day, if you'd like.

Stay in a cool place. Keep the sun out by closing blinds, shades, and curtains. Turn on your air conditioner if you have one. Or use a fan. If your house is too hot, go to a place with air conditioning. Avoid going outside.

Getting Too Hot

If you must go outside

- Before you go out, drink 8 ounces of fluid (if your doctor says it's OK).
- Stay in the shade.
- For every 20 minutes you are outside, drink 6 ounces of fluid.
- Wear a hat with a wide brim.
- Wear sunscreen with an SPF of 15 or more.

Signs of heat sickness

Check off any signs you have.

If you have heat sickness, you may feel:

❏ Confused
❏ Thirsty
❏ Weak or faint

You may have:

❏ Dark yellow or orange urine
❏ Muscle cramps
❏ Skin that is cool and wet (clammy)
❏ Upset stomach

If these signs are not treated, they can lead to a serious form of heat sickness called heatstroke.

Signs of heatstroke

If you have heatstroke, you may:

- ❏ Faint or go into a coma
- ❏ Feel very confused
- ❏ Not sweat at all

You may have:

- ❏ Fever above 104 degrees F
- ❏ Flushed, dry skin
- ❏ Very bad headache
- ❏ Very fast or slow heartbeat

Get help right away

If you have any signs of heatstroke, **call 911**.

Getting Too Cold

As you get older, you are more likely to get too cold. That's because your body makes less heat and doesn't store heat as well. Or, you may not feel the cold as much as you used to. If you get too cold, you could get very sick, or even die.

Protect yourself in cold weather

Avoid alcohol. It makes you lose body heat.

Avoid going outside in cold weather. If you must go out, wear a hat, scarf, and gloves. If your clothes get wet, put on dry ones as soon as you can.

Beware of medicines that make you sleepy. They may not be safe in cold weather. Ask your doctor or pharmacist if it's OK to take them.

Don't smoke. Smoking slows the flow of blood to your hands and feet.

Drink warm fluids. These will help you warm up. But make sure they're warm, and not too hot.

Get enough to eat. Body fat protects you from the cold.

Get ready for winter. Make sure you have a warm place to live. Find out if you can get help paying to insulate or heat your home. Check with your gas or electric company. Or ask at your local senior center.

Keep your home warm. It should be at least 68 degrees F. If need be, just heat the rooms that you use. If you use a space heater, get one that shuts off by itself. Keep it 3 feet away from everything. Don't use the oven, open flames, or barbecue grills inside to heat your home.

Stay active. Your body makes more heat when you move around (see page 133).

Use warm clothes and blankets. Wear extra layers, such as long underwear. Make sure nothing is too tight. For example, wearing more than one pair of socks can cut off blood flow to your feet. This can make your feet get cold quicker. Wear a cap and socks to bed. Put an extra blanket on your bed. If you use an electric blanket, don't tuck it in. And don't put anything on top of it. Don't let your pets sleep on it.

Watch out for these signs

Check off any signs you have, and get help right away:

- ❑ Feel confused or sleepy
- ❑ Shake
- ❑ Purple fingers, toes, and lips
- ❑ Slow heartbeat
- ❑ Slurred speech
- ❑ Your body temperature drops to 96 degrees or lower

Get help right away – Call 911
If you have any of the signs listed above, **call 911**.

Shaking (Tremors)

As you get older, parts of your body are more likely to shake without control. Your hands, head, or voice may shake. Shaky hands can make it hard to eat, drink, write, and get dressed.

Talk with your doctor

If you are concerned about shaking, talk with your doctor. Ask about treatments and tools that can help you at home.

Lessen shaking

Get plenty of sleep, healthy food, and fluid. Limit caffeine (see page 94). Try wearing a heavy bracelet or watch to control the shaking. Do things that relax you.

Make eating easier

Ask someone to cut up your food. Or choose food that you can eat with your hands.

Make drinking easier

Fill your cup halfway, and hold it with 2 hands. Try using a straw or a cup with a lid.

Make writing easier

Print or type instead of using cursive.

Make dressing easier

Choose clothes without buttons, snaps, or zippers. Wear slip-on shoes.

Common Health Problems

4

There are some health problems that you are more likely to have as you get older. Not all seniors will get them. But it's good to know what to look for, and how to handle them. The good news is that some of these problems can be controlled through lifestyle changes, medicines, and other treatments. In some cases, you may be able to prevent them.

Notes

_____

_____

_____

_____

_____

_____

_____

_____

_____

_____

_____

101

Swollen Joints (Arthritis)

As you get older, you are more likely to get arthritis. That's because your joints wear out over time. This common type of arthritis is called osteoarthritis (ahs-tee-oh-ar-THRY-tiss).

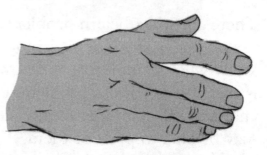

Signs of arthritis

If you have arthritis, your joints may be sore, stiff, and painful. They may be swollen. Plus, your joints may pop and crack when you move them.

Talk with your doctor

If you are concerned about swollen joints, talk with your doctor. Ask about treatments and if you should see an expert.

Lower your symptoms

Choose the right shoes. Look for flat walking shoes with soft soles. They will put less stress on your joints.

Ask your doctor if physical therapy can help with your pain.

Swollen Joints (Arthritis)

Stay active. This may be hard, but it will keep your joints from getting stiff. And it will keep your muscles strong. Strong muscles support your joints better. Exercise for 30 minutes at least 3 times a week (see page 133).

Keep active.

Stay at a healthy weight. Extra weight puts stress on your hips, knees, and ankles.

Alzheimer's Disease

As you get older, you are more likely to have some kind of dementia. Dementia is a wide range of symptoms that include a decline in memory or other thinking skills. This decline is bad enough that it affects the person's ability to do everyday tasks. The most common type of dementia is Alzheimer's. This brain disease makes you forget important things. It also changes the way you think, act, and speak.

In most cases, Alzheimer's builds slowly and gets worse over time. In the end, it causes death. So far, there is no cure for Alzheimer's. But there are treatments.

Signs of Alzheimer's

Check off any signs you have. Bring this list with you on your next visit to the doctor.

If you have Alzheimer's, it may be hard for you to do these things:

❑ **Get around.** You forget how to get home. You put things in strange places. You wander away from home.

❑ **Keep track of time.** You forget the day, month, or year.

❑ **Recall recent events.** You forget things that just happened. But you recall events from long ago.

❑ **Solve problems.** It's hard to shop, follow a recipe, or pay the bills.

❑ **Take care of yourself.** You forget to brush your teeth, take a shower, or put on clean clothes.

❏ **Use language.** It's hard to talk and listen. You ask the same question over and over. You forget your name or the names of family members.

❏ **Handle your feelings.** You often feel sad, upset, and confused. You don't want to go out or do things with other people.

Talk with your doctor

If you are concerned about Alzheimer's, talk with your doctor. Ask about treatments and if you should see an expert. (To learn about normal memory changes, see page 83.) Review your medications that could make your memory worse.

Plan for the future

Plan for the future now, before your memory gets worse. Talk with family members. Tell them what healthcare you want and don't want. (To learn how to make end-of-life choices, see page 60.) Also tell them where you want to live when you can no longer live alone.

Options include:

- Adult day care, in home or daytime care
- Living at home, and getting healthcare (see page 36)
- Living in an assisted living facility or senior apartment
- Living with a family member or friend
- Long-term care facility or full-time care (see page 36)

Get organized

Get a large wall calendar. Mark off the days on it.

Label photos of friends and family members. On the labels, write names, where they live, and what they do.

Make a list of daily tasks. Try to do things at the same time each day.

Make a list of your contacts. Put it by the phone. Or ask someone to put the numbers on speed dial for you (see page 6).

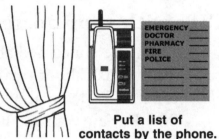

Put a list of contacts by the phone.

Sort closets, cupboards, and drawers. Label them with pictures or words.

Use automatic deposit and bill paying. That way, there's less for you to remember.

Write notes to yourself, and set timers. These can remind you to do things, such as turn off the stove.

Keep track of your medicines. Ask your doctor if your dosing schedule can be made simpler. Make a list of the medicines you take. (To learn how to keep track of your medicines, see page 58.)

Ask friends and family for help

Friends and family members can support you in many ways. They can go on outings with you. They can keep a copy of your house keys, in case you get locked out or lose your keys. They can also help you get organized, pay your bills, shop, cook, and clean.

Don't get lost

When you have Alzheimer's, it's easy to get lost. So have a map and cell phone with you at all times. Keep a copy of your address and phone number. Or get an ID bracelet or necklace. Register with your local police. Contact the Alzheimer's Association help line: (800) 272-3900. Ask about the Safe Return Program and other help.

Depression

As you get older, you are more likely to be depressed. Depression is a mental illness. It changes how you feel, look, and act. It makes it hard to live a normal life. Depression can sometimes be an early sign of Alzheimer's or dementia.

Signs of depression

Check off any signs you have. If you checked off more than 2, talk to your doctor about these signs.

If you are depressed, you may:

❏ Cry for no reason

❏ Eat and sleep too much or too little

❏ Feel sad, tired, and worried all the time for no reason

❏ Have trouble thinking clearly and making choices

❏ Lose interest in things you used to enjoy

❏ Think often about death or killing yourself

Talk with your doctor

If you have any of these signs for more than 2 weeks, talk with your doctor. Ask about treatments and if you should see an expert.

Get the most from your treatment

- Be patient. It may take time to feel better.
- Go to all your office visits, and take your medicine—even if you feel better.

- Learn all you can about depression. Read and ask questions.
- Put off big tasks and choices until you feel better.

Tell your doctor:

- About all the medicines you take
- How well your medicine is working
- How you feel
- If you still feel depressed after 2 weeks of treatment

Improve your mood

Avoid alcohol and illegal drugs. They will make you feel worse.

Eat well and stay active. This will help you feel better (see page 125).

Don't dwell on bad thoughts. Tell yourself, "That's just my depression talking." Replace them with good thoughts.

Get support. Keep in touch with friends and family. Join a support group. If you live alone, think about getting a pet.

Get the right amount of sleep. Try for 8 or 9 hours a night.

Go easy on yourself. Plan a few simple tasks each day. Do things that make you feel good.

Get help right away

If you think you might harm yourself, call your doctor or 911. Or call the National Suicide Prevention Lifeline: (800) 273-TALK. It's open 24 hours a day, 7 days a week.

Leaking Urine (Incontinence)

As you get older, you are more likely to have incontinence (in-KON-tuh-nents). You may leak urine. Or you may be unable to hold your urine at all. There are ways to treat—or even cure—this problem.

Signs of leaking urine

Check off any signs you have. If you checked off any of these, talk to your doctor.

If you have leaking urine, you may:

- ❑ Always feel the urge to pass urine
- ❑ Get up more than 3 times a night to pass urine
- ❑ Have trouble passing urine
- ❑ Leak urine when you cough, sneeze, laugh, lift things, or stand up
- ❑ Pass urine every 1 to 2 hours
- ❑ Wet the bed
- ❑ Wet yourself before you reach the bathroom

Talk with your doctor

If you are concerned about leaking urine, talk with your doctor. Ask about treatments and if you should see an expert.

Leaking Urine (Incontinence)

Stay dry during the day

Fight the urge. If you need to urinate often, try to hold it when you get an urge. It will pass, and you can break the cycle of constant urges.

Avoid caffeine, citrus, and alcohol. They make you pass urine more often.

Get the right amount of fiber. This keeps your bowels regular. Hard stools can cause leaking urine (see page 92).

Never strain. It's bad for your muscles.

Spread out fluids. Don't drink too much at once.

Stay at a healthy weight. Extra weight puts pressure on your bladder.

Take your time. Give your bladder time to empty.

Wear pants with an elastic waist. They're faster to pull down.

Visit the bathroom every 2 hours. Even if you don't feel the need to go. This will help avoid accidents.

Stay dry at night

Empty your bladder right before bed. This will help you stay dry.

Limit fluids. Stop drinking 4 hours before bed.

Sleep near the bathroom. Or keep a bedpan by your bed.

Use night-lights. They will help you find your way to the toilet.

Wear a pad. This will help you stay dry.

Do your Kegels!

Kegel (KAY-guhl) exercises strengthen the pelvic floor muscles. These muscles control the flow of urine. The stronger they are, the more control you will have.

To do one sct of Kegels:

1. Empty your bladder.
2. Sit or lie down.
3. Tighten your pelvic floor muscles. Pretend to stop the flow of urine. Relax the rest of your body. Try doing this on the toilet at first. This will help you feel which muscles you use.
4. Hold for 6 to 8 seconds.
5. Relax for 10 seconds.

Do 10 sets of Kegels, 3 times a day. You can do Kegels while you watch TV, read, or talk on the phone.

Get help right away

Call your doctor right away if you have:

- Back, side, or stomach pain
- Blood in your urine
- Burning feeling when you pass urine
- Chills or fever
- Upset stomach

Weak Bones (Osteoporosis)

As you get older, you are more likely to have osteoporosis (ahs-tee-oh-puh-ROH-suhs). This disease makes your bones thin, weak, and easy to break (brittle). You may break a bone just from lifting something heavy or sneezing. Women are more likely to have brittle bones. But men can have this, too.

Signs of brittle bones

Check off any signs you have.

Both men and women can get brittle bones. Here are some things to watch for that may mean you have osteoporosis:

- ❏ Break bones easily
- ❏ Get back pain
- ❏ Have trouble standing up straight
- ❏ Lose height over time

If you checked any of these boxes, tell your doctor.

Talk with your doctor

If you are concerned about brittle bones, talk with your doctor. Ask if you should get a test to see how dense your bones are. Ask about treatments and if you should see an expert. Ask about taking a supplement.

Make your bones stronger

Do weight-bearing exercises. Walk, climb stairs, and lift light weights (see page 113).

Eat foods with calcium and vitamin D. Dairy foods are a good choice (see page 126).

Limit alcohol and soda. It makes your bones more brittle (see page 146).

Prevent falls. You'll be less likely to break a bone (see page 12).

Quit smoking. It makes your bones more brittle (see page 148).

Get help right away

Call your doctor right away if you fall down or think you broke a bone.

Exercise to stop bone loss.

Enlarged Prostate

The prostate (PRAHS-tayt) is a gland at the bottom of a man's bladder. It gets bigger with age. When the prostate gets bigger, it can press on the urethra. This blocks the flow of urine.

Signs of an enlarged prostate

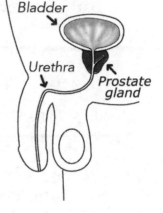

Check off any signs you have.

If you have an enlarged prostate, you may:

- ❏ Dribble urine
- ❏ Feel like there is more urine that won't come out
- ❏ Get a burning feeling when you pass urine
- ❏ Get up more than 2 times a night to pass urine
- ❏ Strain to start the flow of urine

If you checked off any of these boxes, tell your doctor.

Talk with your doctor

If you are concerned about an enlarged prostate, talk with your doctor. Ask about treatments and if you should see an expert.

Get your prostate checked

Ask your doctor when you should have your prostate checked. The doctor will reach into your rectum to check the size of your prostate and feel for lumps.

How to handle an enlarged prostate

- Avoid alcohol and caffeine.
- Do Kegels (see page 112).
- Ejaculate often.
- Pass urine when you first feel the urge.
- Spread out fluids during the day.
- Stop drinking fluids 4 hours before bed. Visit the bathroom every 2 hours when you are awake.

Get help right away

Call your doctor right away if you have:

- Back, side, or stomach pain
- Blood or pus in your urine
- Chills or fever
- Less urine than normal

Heart Attack and Stroke

Your heart, veins, and arteries will change as you get older. Your heart may become a little larger. The walls of your heart get thick and weaker. Your heart may beat faster or slower. Heart valves may not work as well. The arteries may become narrow. This can lead to medical problems called heart disease.

5 Steps to keep your heart in good health

Stop smoking. Using tobacco will damage your heart. It will slow the flow of blood to your body and lungs. Smoking destroys parts of the lungs. You may have cancer or another serious disease from smoking. It will harden your arteries, cause your blood pressure to go up, and make your heart work harder. Secondhand smoke is also harmful. Secondhand smoke is smoke that you breathe when others around you are smoking. When you stop smoking you will lower your chances of having heart disease and cancer. You can find help to stop  smoking by talking to your doctor, searching online, and looking in newspapers. Or go online to smokefree.gov.

Stay at a healthy body weight. Gray hair, wrinkles, and the size and shape of your body will change with aging. The inside of your body will also change. You may need to eat less. If you are overweight, losing weight can make a big difference in your health. Ask your doctor how much weight you should lose.

- Make half of your plate fruits and vegetables.
- Eat less salt.
- Watch for too much sugar in your food.
- Eat foods low in fat.

You also will not want to be too thin. Ask your doctor what your healthy weight should be. There are several apps available on your smartphone that will help you with a healthy diet. A healthy diet will help you have a healthy heart, veins, and arteries.

Stay active. Try to sit less. Do not sit for over an hour. Get up after an hour of sitting, and walk for 2 minutes. Keep moving. Moving keeps muscles and bones healthy. Swim, garden, dance, houseclean, take out the trash, and walk the dog. Moving will help keep your blood pressure normal. It will help you live longer, keep your mind sharp, and you will feel better.

Don't drink a lot of alcohol, wine, or liquor. If you drink, have one drink of alcohol a day or less. Too much alcohol will damage your heart, brain, pancreas, and liver. Over time, alcohol will make your heart muscle weak.

Alcohol may make your heart beat fast. Drinking too much alcohol will lead to high blood pressure. High blood pressure leads to heart disease and stroke. Alcohol will change how medicine works in your body. Medicine mixed with alcohol is poison to your body.

Visit your doctor once a year. Your doctor may decide to see you more often than once a year. Your doctor will want to know your blood pressure and may do other tests to see how your heart is doing.

Blood pressure is the push of blood against the veins, arteries, and heart. Having your blood pressure measured is the only way that you can know what it is. Keep a record of your blood pressure numbers. High blood pressure is when the numbers are higher than they should be. High blood pressure leads to heart disease, heart and kidney failure, and stroke.

Heart Attack

If you are concerned about clogged arteries, talk with your doctor. Ask about treatments and if you should see an expert. Ask if you should get any tests.

A heart attack is when the heart is not getting enough oxygen-rich blood. The blood going to the heart is all at once blocked or cut off. When this happens a part of the heart starts to dic. **Do not wait to get help. Call 911 right away.** Do not drive or have someone else drive you. That way you will have medical people who can begin to save your life on the way to the hospital.

Signs of a heart attack:

- Chest pain in the center of the chest
- Pain in upper body—arms, neck, shoulders
- Having trouble getting your breath
- Sick to your stomach, sweating, lightheaded, or dizzy

Signs of a heart attack are not the same in women as they are in men. Here are signs that a woman may have during a heart attack:

- A woman may say her chest feels tight.
- She may have pain in her jaw or pain that goes down her left arm.
- She may feel tired all the time.
- A woman may wake up at night and have trouble catching her breath.
- She may be dizzy and even black out.
- Her body may swell, especially her ankles, feet, or lower legs.
- Her heart rate may be fast.
- A woman may be sick to her stomach. Or have stomach pain.

Here are signs that a man may have during a heart attack:

- A man may feel pressure in the center of the chest for a few minutes.
- A man may have pain in the chest, shoulders, neck, and arms.
- He may feel faint, sweat, be light-headed, and become short of breath.
- A man may all of a sudden have a fast heartbeat.

Call 911 if you have any **one** of the signs of a heart attack. Get emergency help right away. Do not drive to a hospital.

Angina (an-JIE-nuh)

Angina is chest pain from a low blood flow to the heart. Men may feel angina as squeezing, sour stomach, feeling full, or pain in the center of the chest. Women may feel sick to their stomach, have abdominal or belly pain, have trouble breathing, or feel very tired. They may or may not have chest pain. When angina lasts a few minutes and doesn't go away when you rest or take a medicine for angina, call 911 and get emergency help. Call your doctor if these signs go away after a few minutes.

Stroke

A stroke happens when a blood vessel to the brain gets clogged or bursts. The cells in the brain die when the brain does not get a supply of blood.

Signs that you are having a stroke always occur all of a sudden.

All of a sudden you **can't talk.**

All of a sudden you **are confused.**

All of a sudden you **have pain in one eye.**

All of a sudden you **can't see with one eye.**

All of a sudden you **can't move one side of your body.**

All of a sudden **one side of your face may droop.**

All of a sudden a part of your body becomes **numb, weak, tingles.**

All of a sudden you have **trouble walking.**

All of a sudden you have a **headache that is not the same as other headaches** that you have had.

If you have any **one** of these signs call 911 right away. Do not wait. It is important to get to the hospital right away so treatment can get started.

Remember
Signs of a stroke happen all of a sudden. Don't wait.
Call 911.

Be ready for an emergency

Get ready for a medical emergency. Keep this book in an easy-to-remember place. Keep papers in the book that will be needed in an emergency. Include your advance directive (see page 60). Copies of past medical tests will help. Keep a list of names and phone numbers of people to call. Keep a list of your medicines in the book. Have your insurance cards ready. This will help emergency people get started with your care and treatment.

To learn more:

Go to heart.org to learn more about heart disease and stroke.

Go to lung.org for help to stop smoking.

Go to niaaa.nih.gov/alcohol-health/alcohols-effects-body to learn more about the effects of drinking alcohol.

Diabetes

As you get older, you are more likely to have type 2 diabetes. That means you have too much sugar in your blood.

Over time, high blood sugar can harm many parts of your body. These include your nerves, feet, eyes, and kidneys. High blood sugar can lead to a heart attack, a stroke, or other problems.

Signs of high blood sugar

Check off any signs you have.

If your blood sugar is too high, you may:

- ❏ Feel very thirsty, hungry, or tired
- ❏ Have blurry vision
- ❏ Have sores that heal slowly
- ❏ Lose weight without trying
- ❏ Urinate often

If you checked off any of these boxes, tell your doctor.

Talk with your doctor

If you are concerned about type 2 diabetes, talk with your doctor. Ask about treatments. Ask if you should see an expert. Ask if you should get a blood sugar test.

With type 2 diabetes, signs of high blood sugar tend to come on slowly. You may not notice them until your blood sugar is very high. Your doctor may want to screen you for type 2 diabetes. You may be at risk if you are overweight or have a family history of diabetes.

Lead a healthy lifestyle

- Eat a healthy diet that is low in carbohydrates (see page 126).
- If you smoke, quit (see page 148).
- Limit alcohol (see page 146).
- Lower stress (see page 152).
- Stay active (see page 133).
- Stay at a healthy weight.

Get help right away

If you have trouble keeping your blood sugar in a healthy range, call your doctor.

Staying Well Each Day 5

There are many actions you can take in your daily life to stay well. These lifestyle changes can help you live a longer, better life.

Notes

_____

_____

_____

_____

_____

_____

_____

_____

_____

_____

_____

_____

Eat Right

When you eat right, you get enough of the things your body needs to stay well. And you limit the things that may harm your body. That means you are less likely to get sick or break a bone.

Eating right gives you the energy to do the things you want to do. It keeps your blood pressure and blood sugar in a healthy range. Eating right also helps with depression.

Eat the right amount

Try to stay at a healthy weight. Most seniors need 1,600 to 2,000 calories a day. If you are very active, you may need more. Ask your doctor how many calories are right for you.

In general, eat when you get hungry. Eat slowly. Don't stuff yourself. But don't starve yourself either.

Eat the right foods

Make sure you get all the things your body needs. You'll have better health and more energy. For tips on how to make healthy choices, go to ChooseMyPlate.gov.

Have these each day:

Beans and peas. These are full of protein, vitamins, and minerals. They are also high in fiber. Watch out for added salt in canned beans.

Fruits. These are packed with vitamins and fiber. Choose whole fruit instead of juice. Watch out for added sugar in canned fruit.

Fish, lean meat, and poultry. These contain protein, vitamins, and minerals. The fat in fish is good for you. But the fat in meat and poultry can harm your health. Watch out for added salt in cured meat, such as bacon or sausage.

Nonfat and low-fat dairy. They contain protein and minerals. But dairy fat can harm your health. So choose skim or 1% milk and yogurt. Look for part-skim cheese.

Vegetables. These are great source of vitamins, minerals, and fiber. Choose whole vegetables. Watch out for added salt in some canned vegetables.

Whole grains. These contain vitamins, minerals, and fiber. Try to make at least half of your grains whole grains. Look for 100% whole wheat bread and pasta. Try oatmeal for breakfast.

Limit these:

Eggs. These contain protein, vitamins, and minerals. But they are also high in cholesterol, which can harm your heart. No more than one egg per day.

Healthy fat. This is good for your heart. But it is also high in calories. It is found in vegetable oils, such as olive and canola. It is also found in avocados and salmon.

Nuts and seeds. These are a great source of protein, fiber, and healthy fat. They are full of vitamins and minerals. But they are also high in calories.

Avoid these:

Alcohol. This can affect your health in a number of ways. It may also affect how well your medicines work.

Salt (also called sodium). Too much can raise your blood pressure. It can also lead to swelling in your legs. Try not to add salt to your food. Watch out for added salt in prepared foods, such as soy sauce, mustard, and olives. Restaurant food, especially fast food, can be very high in salt.

Sugar. This can raise your blood sugar. It is also high in calories. Try not to add sugar to your food. Watch out for added sugar in prepared foods, such as sodas, cereal, cakes, and cookies.

Unhealthy fat. This is bad for your heart. And it's high in calories. So avoid saturated fat. It's found in animal products, such as full-fat dairy and fatty cuts of meat. Also avoid trans fat. It's found in many fried foods and packaged desserts.

Read the label

Before you buy a prepared food, read the Nutrition Facts label. The label tells how much is in one serving, and how many servings are in the package. For each serving, the label lists the number of calories. It also gives the amount of protein, fat, sugar, and other nutrients.

Nutrition Facts

Serving Size 1/2 square (14g)
Servings Per Container 16

Amount Per Serving

Calories 70

Calories from Fat 40

	% Daily Value*
Total Fat 4.5g	7%
Saturated Fat 2.5g	13%
Cholesterol 0mg	0%
Sodium 0mg	0%
Total Carbohydrate 8g	3%
Dietary Fiber 1g	4%
Sugars 7g	
Protein <1g	

Vitamin A 0%	•	Vitamin C 0%	
Calcium 0%	•	Iron 4%	

*Percent Daily Values are based on a 2,000 calorie diet. Your daily values may be higher or lower depending on your calorie needs:

		Calories	2,000	2,500
Total Fat	Less than		65g	80g
Sat Fat	Less than		20g	25g
Cholest	Less than		300mg	300mg
Sodium	Less than		2,400mg	2,400mg
Total Carb			300g	375g
Fiber			25g	30g

INGREDIENTS: SEMI-SWEET CHOCOLATE (CHOCOLATE, SUGAR, COCOA BUTTER, SOY LECITHIN [EMULSIFIER], VANILLA EXTRACT, MILK SOLIDS).

1 OZ. SQUARE OF CHOCOLATE

Get your fruits and vegetables

Half of your food should be fruits and vegetables. Here are some ways to fit them into your diet.

- Buy fruits and vegetables that are in season. Or choose frozen fruits and vegetables. They may taste better. And they often cost less.

- Have fresh fruit for dessert. If you want, add a small dab of whipped cream on top. Or sprinkle a little cinnamon on top.

- Learn new ways to cook and season your vegetables. Look at magazines or websites for recipes.

- Make smoothies. Choose fresh or frozen fruits and vegetables. Blend them with an equal amount of milk or 100% juice.

- Put vegetables on your sandwich. Try them with pasta and rice. Or put them in soups, stews, and sauces. If you don't like vegetables, mince or puree them.

- Top yogurt or cereal with fresh fruit.

- Try new fruits and vegetables. You might find one you like!

- Wash and cut up fruits and vegetables that you like. Put them in your refrigerator for an easy snack. Keep fruit in a bowl.

Get the right amount of fiber

Fiber helps keep your bowels regular. It lowers your blood sugar. It is good for your heart and helps prevent colon cancer.

Eat cereals that have the right amount of fiber

Seniors should eat fiber every day. Ask your doctor how much you need. Women need about 21 grams of fiber each day. Men need about 30 grams each day. You can get it from fruits, vegetables, and whole grains, such as oatmeal. Fiber is also found in nuts, seeds, beans, and peas.

Add fiber to your diet slowly. If you eat too much at once, you may have gas, bloating, or cramps.

Be a healthy cook

The way you cook can affect how healthy your food is. To limit fat, steam or grill your vegetables. Broil, bake, grill, or roast meat. Remove the fat and skin before serving.

Make sauces that are low in salt, sugar, and fat. Try using lemon juice, herbs, and spices.

Handle challenges

For many of us, eating right is hard. Here are some ways to deal with it.

Challenge: I have trouble shopping.

- Ask a family member, friend, or volunteer to take you shopping. Or ask if they will shop for you.

- Find out if your local grocery store delivers. Or order food online.

- Look into Meals On Wheels. Call (888) 998-6325. Or go to Mowaa.org.

Ask for help shopping.

- If you have trouble paying for food, ask about food banks.

Challenge: I have trouble cooking.

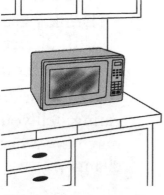

Use a microwave oven.

- Buy cooked foods that you can take home.

- Find out if your local senior center has a meal program. Ask if they will bring meals to your home.

- Keep frozen dinners on hand. Heat them up when you don't feel like cooking. But watch out for extra salt in these meals. And be careful not to burn yourself.

- Look into Meals On Wheels. Call 1-888-998-6325. Or go to Mowaa.org.

- Move to a place where someone else does the cooking.

- Use a microwave oven. Take care not to burn yourself.

- When you do cook, make a large batch. Freeze what you don't use. Write a note on the outside telling what is inside and when you froze it. Freeze in single servings.

Challenge: I have trouble chewing.

- Puree your fruits and vegetables. Or put them in a smoothie.

- Try soft foods, such as rice, pasta, oatmeal, and yogurt.

- If you often have trouble chewing, tell your dentist. You may need dental work or help using your dentures.

Challenge: I don't feel like eating.

- Add more herbs and spices to your food.

- Be more active.

- Choose foods with more calories.
- Cut out caffeine.
- Drink a glass of red wine with dinner.
- Eat with other people.

Eat with family or friends.

If you often don't feel like eating, tell your doctor. You may have a health problem. Or your medicines may need to change.

Challenge: I get an upset stomach when I eat.

- Avoid foods that upset your stomach. Watch out for food high in acids or fats.
- Eat smaller meals.
- Make sure the food you eat is fresh.

See your doctor if your stomach is often upset.

If you often get an upset stomach, tell your doctor. You may have a health problem.

Do you need vitamins?

It's best to get the things your body needs from food. But if you have trouble meeting your needs, pills may be an option.

Ask your doctor if you should take any vitamins, minerals, or supplements. If the answer is yes, ask what to take and how to take it. Also find out if these pills will affect how your medicine works.

Stay Active – Get Fit

Staying active helps you stay well in many ways. It gives you more energy and makes you feel good.

Exercise can:

- Give you better balance
- Help you lose weight or stay at a healthy weight
- Help you sleep well
- Keep your blood pressure and blood sugar in a healthy range
- Keep your memory sharp
- Strengthen your heart, lungs, muscles, and bones

Get started

It's never too late to get active. Here's how to get started.

Talk with your doctor. Before you start to get active, talk with your doctor. Ask what kind of exercise is right for you and how much you should do. Most seniors can do 30 minutes or more of exercise at least 5 days a week. Find out if there are any things you should avoid.

Choose a way to be active. There are many options, so find something that you enjoy. Walk, dance, or swim. Try a video or a fitness class. Play golf or tennis with a friend. Try tai chi to improve your balance or yoga to get more flexible.

Make a plan. Decide what you will do and how much you will do. Also decide when you will do it.

Start out slowly. Get more active over time. This will give your body a chance to get stronger. You have less chance to get hurt.

Dress for fitness

Check off the tips you try.

Let air in
Firm back
Room for toes
Raised heel
Good arch
Sturdy sole

- ❏ **Choose the right shoes.** Look for shoes that fit well and feel good. Make sure they lace up and grip well. Try inserts for extra padding. Always wear socks.

- ❏ **Dress in layers.** Take off layers as you warm up. Choose stretchy fabrics, such as spandex, that don't soak up and hold sweat.

- ❏ **Wear a helmet.** If you bike, always wear a helmet. The helmet should fit snugly and cover the top of your forehead.

Eat and drink for fitness

Check off the tips you try.

Exercise 30 minutes 5 days a week

- ❏ **Avoid alcohol.** Don't drink alcohol before or after you exercise.

- ❏ **Drink enough water.** Drink a glass of water before and after you exercise. If your urine is dark yellow or orange, you are not drinking enough.

134

❑ **Eat lightly.** Avoid eating a big meal before you exercise. Instead, choose something light, such as yogurt.

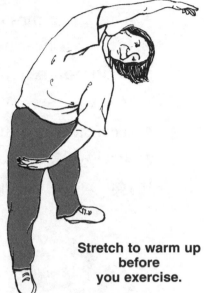

Stretch to warm up before you exercise.

Use fitness sense

Check off the tips you try.

❑ **Breathe normally.** Breathe in and out. Don't hold your breath when you exercise.

❑ **Stay cool.** If it's hot outside, find a place with air conditioning.

❑ **Warm up.** Before you start, warm up for about 10 minutes. You can walk slowly, march in place, or swing your arms.

❑ **Cool down.** After you finish, let your body cool down for 30 minutes. Do easy stretches. Don't rush to the shower.

❑ **Exercise before 6 p.m.** If you work out later, you may have trouble sleeping.

❑ **Have a fitness buddy.** This can make fitness more fun. You are more likely to stick to your plan. Plus, you and your friend can watch out for each other.

❑ **Do chair exercises** if you have trouble standing.

Know when NOT to be active

Do **not** exercise if you have any of these signs:

• Chest pain or pressure

- Fever or infection
- Pain or cramps
- Very fast heartbeat

Also do **not** exercise if you:

- Are very sweaty or out of breath
- Feel sick to your stomach
- Feel weak or dizzy

If you need help right away, call 911.

Take Good Care of Your Mouth

Taking good care of your mouth boosts your overall health. If your mouth is not healthy, you are more likely to:

- Get pneumonia
- Have diabetes (see page 123)
- Have heart problems (see page 117)
- Lose too much weight

Keep Your Teeth and Gums Healthy

Tooth and gum problems are common. That's because the mouth has a lot of germs.

Tooth decay

Tooth decay is damage to the outer surface of your teeth. It is caused by plaque. Plaque is a film of bacteria that builds up on your teeth.

Plaque makes acids that eat away at your teeth. Over time, these acids may make a hole (cavity) in your teeth.

Tooth decay isn't just for kids. It can happen at any age, as long as you have natural teeth.

Gum disease

Gum disease is an infection of your gums. It happens when plaque builds up along and under your gum line.

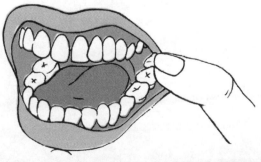

There are 2 types of gum disease:

Early gum disease (gingivitis)

If you have early gum disease, your gums are red and swollen. They bleed easily.

You can reverse early gum disease by taking good care of your mouth. If not treated, it can lead to advanced gum disease.

Advanced gum disease (periodontitis)

If you have advanced gum disease, your gums pull away from your teeth. This creates gaps (pockets) that become infected.

Your dentist can help you treat advanced gum disease. If not treated, it can destroy the bones, gums, and tissues that support your teeth. Over time, your teeth may get loose and need to be removed.

If you have diabetes

You are more likely to get gum disease. In turn, gum disease can make it hard to control your blood sugar (see page 123).

Take Good Care of Your Mouth

Keep your mouth clean

That's the best way to keep your teeth and gums healthy. To keep your mouth clean:

Brush your teeth at least 2 times each day. Brushing removes plaque from the surface of your teeth and gums.

Floss your teeth at least one time each day. Flossing removes plaque from **between** your teeth.

Brush your teeth the right way

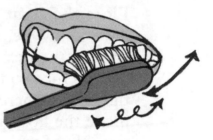

- **Choose the right toothbrush.** Use one that has soft bristles and fits your mouth well. If you have arthritis in your shoulder or hand, think about using an electric toothbrush.

- **Choose the right toothpaste.** Use one with fluoride. Fluoride helps prevent tooth decay.

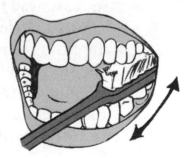

- **Brush the right way.** Hold your toothbrush at a slight angle. Aim the bristles at your gum line. Move the brush gently back and forth. Brush every surface of your teeth, plus your tongue. Take the time to do a good job.

- **Keep your toothbrush clean.** Rinse your toothbrush after each use. Let it air-dry in an upright position away from anyone else's brush.

- **Change your toothbrush often.** Replace it when the bristles fray. That's about every 3 months. If you use an electric toothbrush, replace the head.

Take Good Care of Your Mouth

Floss your teeth the right way

- **Choose the right floss.** If your teeth are close together, use skinny floss. If you have some space between your teeth, use wider floss. Is floss hard to use? Talk to your dentist about other tools to use.

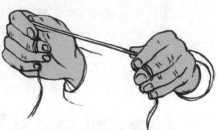

- **Floss the right away.** You may have to saw gently back and forth to slide the floss between your teeth. Once you are through the tight spot where your teeth touch, move the floss up and down on the side of each tooth. Take the time to do a good job.

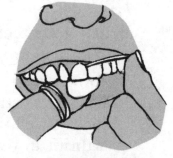

- **Use plenty of floss.** About 18 inches will give you a good grip. An easy way to use floss is to tie it into a circle. Wind most of the floss around each middle finger. Then hold a small amount between each thumb and forefinger. After you floss each tooth, move to a clean spot on the floss circle.

Other ways to keep teeth and gums healthy

- Eat a healthy diet (see page 126).
- If you smoke or chew tobacco, quit (see page 148).
- Limit sugar.

Take Good Care of Your Mouth

Visit your dentist

Tell the dental staff about any medicines you take and any health problems you have. They will clean and check your teeth and gums. They may give you a fluoride treatment to protect your teeth from decay. They may ask you to use a fluoride gel or mouth rinse at home.

Know when to call your dentist's office

Call the office if your **gums**:

- Are red, tender, or swollen
- Are starting to pull away from your teeth
- Bleed when you brush or floss

Call the office if your **teeth**:

- Are loose
- Don't line up the way they used to
- Hurt when you drink something hot or cold

Also call if you have bad breath that lasts, or if your mouth tastes funny.

If You Wear Dentures

Even if you wear dentures, you still need to take good care of your mouth. In fact, you have some extra jobs to do.

Clean your mouth at least <u>2 times</u> each day

Follow these steps:

1. Take your dentures out.
2. Brush any natural teeth you have.

3. Clean your tongue and palate (roof of your mouth) with gauze or a soft toothbrush.

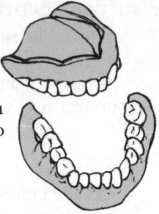

Keep your dentures clean

- **Rinse your dentures <u>each</u> <u>time</u> you eat.** Run water over your dentures to clean off any food.

- **Scrub your dentures at least <u>one</u> <u>time</u> each day.** Use denture cleaner or mild soap. Choose a denture brush or soft toothbrush. Scrub gently.

- **Handle your dentures with care.** Be careful not to bend or break your dentures. Place a towel in the sink so they won't break if you drop them.

- **Soak your dentures overnight.** Most dentures need to stay moist. Ask your dentist what type of liquid to soak them in.

- **Rinse your dentures before you put them back in your mouth.** Do not swallow soaking liquids.

- **Check for sores or white spots on your gums under your dentures.** This could be fungus. See your dentist right away.

Visit your dentist

The dental staff will check and clean your dentures. They will make sure your dentures fit well.

Know when to call your dentist's office.

Call the office if your dentures get loose. Loose dentures can make your gums sore and cause infection.

How to Handle Dry Mouth

When you have dry mouth, you don't have enough spit to keep your mouth wet. Dry mouth makes you more likely to get tooth decay.

Signs of dry mouth

Check off any signs you have.

If you have dry mouth:

- ❑ You may have trouble chewing, eating, swallowing, or talking.
- ❑ If you wear dentures, they may not fit well. They may rub against your gums and make them sore.
- ❑ Your tongue may stick to the roof of your mouth.

Talk with your doctor or dentist

If you are concerned about dry mouth, talk with your doctor or dentist. Ask about treatments.

Keep your mouth wet

- Chew gum with no sugar in it.
- Suck hard candy with no sugar in it.
- Use fake spit. You'll find it in many drugstores.

Watch for Mouth (Oral) Cancer

It's important to spot mouth cancer early. That's because treatment works best at that stage.

Your dentist should check you for mouth cancer. But you should watch for it, too.

Signs of mouth cancer

Check off any signs you have.

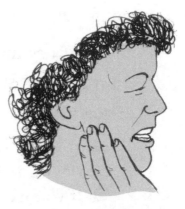

If you have mouth cancer, you may have:

- ❏ A feeling that something is caught in your throat
- ❏ Numbness in your tongue or other parts of your mouth
- ❏ Pain in one ear without hearing loss
- ❏ Sore or thick area in your mouth, lip, or throat
- ❏ Lump in your mouth, lip, or throat
- ❏ Swelling in your jaw
- ❏ Trouble chewing or swallowing
- ❏ Trouble moving your jaw or tongue
- ❏ White or red area in your mouth

If you have any of these signs for more than 2 weeks, talk with your doctor or dentist. Ask about treatments and if you should see an expert. Ask if you should get any tests.

Keep in mind: These signs can be caused by problems other than cancer. But it's good to get them checked out, just in case.

Lower your risk of mouth cancer
- If you smoke or chew tobacco, quit (see page 148).
- Limit alcohol (see page 146).

How to Pay for Dental Care

Medicare doesn't pay for most dental care. But there are ways to get dental care at a lower cost.

If you need your teeth cleaned

Many dental hygiene schools run clinics. Students there clean your teeth at a lower cost. Trained dental staff watch over them.

To learn more about this option, contact your local dental hygiene school. Or go to: adha.org/education-careers.

If you need other care, such as fillings

Many dental schools run clinics. Students there care for your teeth at a lower cost. Trained dentists watch over them.

To learn more about this option, contact your local dental school. Or go to: ada.org/en/coda/find-a-program/ search-dental-programs/dds-dmd-programs.

The U.S. government runs health centers. Some of these centers have dental clinics. You pay them based on your income. **In many states, Medicaid pays for dental care.** To learn more about this option, go to: findahealthcenter.hrsa.gov.

Think About What You Put in Your Body

Too much alcohol can harm your health. So can too much medicine. And smoking is one of the worst things you can do to your health.

Know how alcohol affects you

As you get older, alcohol may affect you more. It can affect the way your medicines work. When you drink, you are more likely to fall down or crash your car. You forget things and get confused more.

Limit how much you drink

Drinking may not be OK with some of your medicines. Check first with your doctor or pharmacist. In general, it is safe to have:

- 1 drink per day for most women
- 2 drinks per day for most men

1 drink means:

- 5 ounces of wine, OR
- 1½ ounces of hard liquor, OR
- 12 ounces of beer

One drink of alcohol is:

5 ounces
of wine

or

1 1/2 ounces
of hard liquor
(booze)

or

12 ounces
of beer

Think About What You Put in Your Body

Don't mix alcohol and medicine

Mixing alcohol and medicine can harm you. Ask your doctor or pharmacist about alcohol and your medicines. And never drink and drive. Even one drink is too much.

DO NOT MIX !

Causes of a drinking problem

You may find yourself drinking more when you stop working, or after the death of a friend or family member. You may also drink more when you have poor health or too little money. If you come to rely on drinking, you may have a drinking problem (alcoholism).

Signs of a drinking problem

Check off any signs you have.

You may have a drinking problem if you:

- ❑ Drink alone more often than you used to
- ❑ Drink to deal with your feelings
- ❑ Enjoy food less
- ❑ Feel angry or grumpy when you don't drink
- ❑ Get drunk more than 3 or 4 times a year
- ❑ Gulp drinks fast
- ❑ Have health, social, or money problems from drinking
- ❑ Hurt yourself or someone else when you drink
- ❑ Lie to hide how much you drink

If you checked any of these signs, talk to your doctor.

Think About What You Put in Your Body

Beware of medicine abuse

Medicine abuse happens when you take too much medicine on purpose. This can harm your health.

It is more common to abuse drugs that:

- Ease pain, such as Percocet and Vicodin
- Make you less anxious, such as Xanax and Valium
- Make you sleep

But medicine abuse can happen with any drug.

Use your medicines the right way

- Never drink alcohol with your medicines. You could get very sick.
- Never use a drug that was prescribed for someone else.
- Take your medicines the way your doctor told you to. Take the right amount at the right time. If you are not sure how to take a medicine, ask your doctor or pharmacist.
- Tell your doctor about all the medicines you take.

If you smoke, quit

Smoking is one of the worst things you can do to your health. It makes it harder to breathe and stay active. And you have more chance of getting other health problems.

If you smoke, you are more likely to have:

- Heart attack
- Lung cancer
- Stroke

If you quit, you can undo much of the harm caused by smoking. Talk with your doctor about how to quit. Or go to smokefree.gov.

Find New Ways to Enjoy Sex

As you get older, your feelings about sex may change. You may want sex less. And it may take longer to get ready to have sex.

If you are a woman. The level of your sex hormones goes down. Your vagina may feel sore. The vagina's muscles get weaker, and the walls get thinner. Your vagina may be dry. This can make sex painful.

If you are a man. You may have trouble getting or keeping an erection. You may make less semen, or none at all.

Health and medicines affect sex

If you have arthritis, diabetes, or heart disease, it may be harder to have sex. They can also make you want it less. Some medicines cause the same problems.

Surgery for prostate cancer can make it harder to have an erection. Smoking cuts blood flow to the penis.

Ways to get in the mood
- Go to bed nude.
- Unplug the phone.
- Play soft music.
- Read a sexy book.
- Take a warm bath.
- Turn off the TV and the computer.
- Watch a sexy movie.

You can still enjoy sex

Be careful about ads for sex products. They are trying to sell you things.

Learn all you can. Read about sex for seniors.

Comfort is important. Try other sex positions. Use pillows to support your weight.

Take your time. Getting ready for sex may take longer than it used to.

Talk with your doctor. Tell your doctor about any problems you have with sex. Ask if your health problems or medicines are causing them. Find out what you can do to make sex better.

Talk with your partner. Tell your partner what feels good to you. Ask what your partner likes. Talk about ways to make sex better.

Try other ways to have sex. Use your fingers or mouth to please your partner. Or touch yourself.

If you are a woman:

Try using lubricants.

Talk with your doctor about female hormones, such as creams or pills.

Use lubricant during sex.

If you are a man:

Talk with your doctor about medicines that help you get or keep an erection.

Have safe sex

Seniors can get sexually transmitted diseases (STDs). These are also called sexually transmitted infections (STIs). Unless you are in a committed relationship, use a condom or dental dam.

Other ways to be close

Sex is not the only way to be close to your partner.

- Dance to your special song.
- Give small gifts, or send love notes.
- Go on a date.
- Hug, kiss, and hold hands.
- Massage your partner's back, feet, or hands.
- Smile, or say something kind.

Show your love.

Take Care of Your Feelings

Feelings such as stress, worry, anger, and sadness can have a big effect on your health. So be sure to take care of your feelings.

Stay in touch

We all need other people. Being socially connected helps our memory and our health. Call or visit with friends, family members, and neighbors. Want to meet new people? Join a club, take a class, or get a part-time job.

If you can't leave home, invite people over. Or connect by phone or online. A pet can also be a great friend.

Keep learning

You're never too old to learn. Learning helps keep your mind sharp. Plus, it's fun. So take a class, read, travel, or go to talks. Ask about free events at your local library and senior center.

Keep laughing

You're never too old to laugh, either. So watch funny TV shows and movies. Play silly games, and read funny books.

Have fun.

Take Care of Your Feelings

Have friends.

Do things you enjoy

Try to do something you enjoy each day. You may like to garden, fish, play golf, travel, share a meal, or walk with a friend. You may even find something new that you love!

Talk about your feelings

Sometimes just talking about your feelings can make you feel better. Plus, it can help you solve some problems. Talk about your feelings with someone you trust. This could be a friend, family member, or doctor.

Ask for help when you need it

From time to time, you may need help with cooking, cleaning, or shopping. You may need a ride to the doctor. Feel free to ask friends and family for help. Try to accept help when they offer it. Offer to help others if you can.

Relax ... 1, 2, 3, 4

Need to unwind? Take these steps:

1. Put your feet up.
2. Close your eyes.
3. Breathe slowly and deeply.
4. Empty your mind.

Paying for Healthcare 6

Healthcare can be very costly. Before you get healthcare, think about how you will pay for it.

Find out:

- How much you will have to pay
- If your health plan covers it
- If your doctor needs to approve your care ahead of time
- If your health plan needs to approve your care ahead of time

Notes

_____

_____

_____

_____

_____

_____

_____

_____

155

Make Sense of
Medicare Parts A and B

Medicare is a health insurance plan for seniors. The U.S. government runs it. Original Medicare has 2 parts: A and B.

Part A covers hospital care. It helps pay for care in hospitals and long-term care facilities. (But it doesn't pay for long-term care.) It also pays for home healthcare and hospice care.

Medicare card.

You can get Part A for free if you or your spouse paid taxes while you worked. If you don't get Part A for free, you may be able to buy it.

Part B covers healthcare. It pays for doctor visits and testing. It also pays for ambulance services and some medical supplies.

There is a monthly fee for Part B. This fee is called your premium (PREE-mee-um). In most cases, this fee comes out of your Social Security checks. If you opted out of Part B before, you may need to pay more.

How to get Parts A and B

If you get Social Security. You **do not** need to sign up for Parts A and B. You will be covered starting on the first day of the month you turn 65. You will get papers in the mail a few months before your 65th birthday.

Make Sense of Medicare Parts A and B

If you do NOT get Social Security.
You **do** need to sign up for Parts A and B. Apply 3 months before you turn 65. You can apply online at SSA.gov. Or you can apply in person at your local Social Security office. Call to schedule a meeting.

How to use Parts A and B

Use any healthcare provider that takes Medicare. Then send the bill to Medicare. You may not get back the whole amount. If you use a provider who **does not** take Medicare, you may need to pay the bill in full. Make sure you ask your healthcare provider if they accept Medicare before you have your visit.

Know your costs

You may need to pay:

- **Deductible.** That's the amount you pay each year before Medicare begins to pay.

- **Coinsurance.** That's your share, or percentage, of the cost for care.

- **Co-pay.** That's a set amount you pay at each visit.

Before you get routine healthcare, find out how much you will need to pay. But if you need care right away, don't wait.

Use your Medicare Summary Notice (MSN)

You will get an MSN in the mail every 3 months. This lists all the care billed to Parts A and B. It shows what Medicare paid and what you may owe.

Make good usc of your MSN. Read it carefully. Compare your receipts and bills to your MSN.

If Medicare did NOT cover an item

Call your provider. Make sure they asked Medicare to cover it. Or see if you have other insurance that will cover it.

If you think Medicare made a mistake, you can appeal. See your MSN for advice. Many senior organizations will help you file an appeal if you need help.

Make Sense of
Medicare Part C

Private companies run Medicare Part C. They have a contract with Medicare. Part C is also called Medicare Advantage. You have to see doctors who have a contract with the Medicare Advantage Health Plan.

Like Parts A and B, Part C can help pay for:

- Ambulance services and some medical supplies
- Care in hospitals and long-term care facilities (but it doesn't pay for long-term care)
- Doctor visits and testing
- Home healthcare and hospice care

Most Part C plans also cover other care, such as prescription drugs.

How to get Part C

In order to get a Part C plan, you must sign up for it. Part C plans are available only in certain parts of the U.S. If you sign up for a Part C plan, you can no longer use Part A or B.

What you <u>may like</u> about Part C

Part C plans may cost you less and cover more care than Parts A and B. Part C plans may also make less paperwork for you than Parts A and B.

What you <u>may not like</u> about Part C

<u>Part C plans may:</u>

- Change from year to year
- Make you choose from a list of providers
- Not be available near you
- Require a referral to see experts

Shop around

There are many Part C plans. Each plan has its own benefits, costs, and rules. These change from year to year.

Before you sign up for a plan, learn all you can about the plans near you. Compare them to each other. Also compare them to Parts A and B.

Find out:

- How much you would pay
- If it covers your prescription drugs
- If it has a list of providers you have to choose from
- If your doctor is on its list
- What care it covers

Make Sense of
Medicare Part D

Medicare Part D helps you pay for prescription drugs.

How to get Part D

You can sign up for a Part D plan when you start getting Parts A and B. After that, you can join, switch, or drop a Part D plan between October 15 and December 7 each year. In some cases, you may be able to change your Part D plan at other times.

Shop around

There are many Part D plans. Each plan has its own benefits, costs, and rules. These change from year to year.

Before you sign up for a plan, learn all you can about the plans near you. Compare them to each other. Also compare them to Part C plans.

Find out:

- How much you would pay
- If it covers your prescription drugs
- If you can get your drugs by mail
- If your local pharmacy is on the plan's list

To Learn More About Medicare

To get the most from Medicare, learn all you can.

Go to Medicare.gov

Here you can:

- Apply for Medicare
- Find Medicare and Medigap plans
- Find providers
- Get booklets such as "Your Guide to Medicare Prescription Drug Coverage" and "Medicare & You"
- Get forms
- Log in to learn facts that are just for you

Call Medicare

If you have questions, call:

1-800-633-4227 (main number)

1-877-486-2048 (TTY)

Get free advice about Medicare

Contact the State Health Insurance Assistance Program (SHIP). Go to shiptalk.org to learn how.

More ways to learn about Medicare

Ask for help at your local hospital, library, senior center, or Social Security office.

A Note on the Affordable Care Act

The Affordable Care Act (ACA) became law in 2010. If you have Medicare, you may get more care for less money.

Under the ACA, you can have a free wellness visit each year. And some cancer tests are free.

If you are in the "donut hole" for prescription drugs, you get a discount. The donut hole is the part of your drug costs that you must pay for each year. By the year 2020, the donut hole will be closed.

Other Ways to
Pay for Healthcare

Medicare will not cover all your healthcare costs. Here are some other ways to pay for healthcare.

Find out if you can get Medicaid

Medicaid is a state and federal program. It pays some healthcare costs that Medicare does not.

You may be able to get Medicaid if you have low income or you are disabled. Each state has its own rules for who can get Medicaid and what it covers. To learn what Medicaid pays for, and to apply for Medicaid, call your local office.

Many seniors believe you cannot get Medicaid if you own a home. This is not true. Most states decide if you can get Medicaid based on your monthly income and how much you have in the bank.

Buy Medigap insurance

Private companies run Medigap plans. They pay some healthcare costs that Medicare Parts A and B do not. But they do not cover prescription drugs.

Medigap is also called supplemental insurance. If you have a Part C plan, you do not need Medigap.

Shop around for Medigap or supplemental insurance.

Other Ways to Pay for Healthcare

Shop around

Before you sign up for a Medigap plan, learn all you can about the plans in your state. Compare them to each other. Also compare them to Part C plans.

Find out:

- How much you would pay
- If it covers deductibles and co-pays
- If it has a list of providers
- If your doctor is on its list
- What care it covers

We Wish You Well

We hope this book has helped you take charge of your health. You have a right to know how to get and pay for healthcare and how to stay safe and well. We wish you good health!

Word List

A

- abuse—Harm that is done to a person. Can be things like hitting, stealing, taunting, or not taking care of a person.

- advance directive—A legal paper on which you write what you want for medical care if you get too ill to speak for yourself. This paper may also list someone that you choose to make decisions for you if you are unable to make them. Each state has its own laws regarding advance directives.

- Affordable Care Act (ACA)—The national healthcare reform law enacted in March 2010. It provides all U.S. citizens with access to health insurance.

- AIDS (Acquired Immune Deficiency Syndrome)—A disease passed by sex or IV drug users that causes bad sickness and death.

- allergy—Getting sick (itching, sneezing, hives, hard breathing, or even unconsciousness) from something such as medicine, food, plant, dust, or other things.

- alcoholic—A person who cannot control how much alcohol he or she drinks.

- Alzheimer's disease—A disease of the brain that causes people to forget things.

- appeal—A right to ask Medicare about something that they did not pay for when you thought it was covered by Medicare.

- appetite—The normal desire for food.

- appointment—The time of day that you visit the doctor or clinic.
- arthritis—Pain, stiffness, or swelling in the joints.
- atherosclerosis—A condition where plaque builds up and clogs your arteries.

C

- calcium—A mineral found in bones and teeth. Makes them strong.
- carbon monoxide—A gas that has no color and no smell.
- cataract—The lens in the eye becomes cloudy and the person cannot see.
- cervix—The neck-like part of the womb (woman's organ).
- clinic—Another word for a doctor's office.
- cholesterol—A form of fat that is a major cause of heart disease in men and women. It clogs the flow of blood.
- coinsurance—The percentage of a medical or dental cost that you will have to pay.
- colonoscopy—Test that allows your doctor to see inside your rectum and colon.
- co-pay—The set amount you pay for medical or dental services.
- concentrate—Thinking about one thing.
- condom—A latex cover put on a hard penis before sex. It prevents pregnancy and many sexually transmitted diseases. Also called a rubber.
- constipated—Unable to have a bowel movement (pass solid waste from the body).

Word List

- coverage—Type of insurance.
- credentials—License and papers that shows someone can legally practice medicine or provide healthcare services.

D

- deductible—The amount you have to pay for healthcare.
- dementia—Loss of brain function.
- depression—Feeling sad all the time.
- diet—Food that you eat every day.
- disease—Sickness or an illness.
- diabetes—A disease where there is too much sugar in the blood.
- disability—Not able to work due to illness or injury.
- donut hole—Coverage gap for prescription drugs under Medicare Part D.

E

- emergency—A medical problem that may cause lasting harm or death. Like heavy bleeding or trouble breathing.
- emotional—Feelings.
- erection—A hard penis.
- ejaculate—When semen comes out of the penis while having sex.
- exercise—Body movement that makes the heart beat and breathing go faster.

F

- farsightedness—A vision condition where distant objects are easier to see than closer objects.

- fiber—Part of plants like fruits, vegetables, and grains that the body does not digest or use. When eaten helps the body get rid of waste.

- frail—Loss of muscle and strength.

G

- generic—Lower-cost drugs and other products that have no brand name.

- geriatricians—Doctors who care for seniors.

- glaucoma—A disease in the eye where the pressure inside the eye is too high and will not let the eye work.

H

- hormone—Body juices made in the body to do certain things.

- hospice—A team of people who give care and services to a person and their family when the person is nearing the end of their life.

I

- illness—Having a sickness or a disease and in poor health.

- incontinence—Unable to control your bladder.

- infection—Sickness caused by germs you cannot see. An infection can happen inside the body or on the skin. Signs of infection are redness, heat, pain and liquid, or pus oozing from the skin.

- inpatient—You get admitted to a hospital, which means you get care there and stay overnight or longer.

Word List

L

- living will—A type of advance directive. A legal paper that tells your wishes at the end of your life for medical treatment if you cannot talk.

M

- macular degeneration—The center part of the eye crumbles, and there is a slow loss of eyesight.

- mammogram—An x-ray of the breast to check for cancer.

- medical record—A file that holds papers about one patient's health. Also called patient's chart.

- Medicare—The healthcare part of the Social Security program for people over the age of 65. Part A covers hospital care. Part B covers doctor care and other services that you receive when you are not a hospital patient.

- Medicare Advantage Plan—A Medicare plan under Part C offered by health insurance companies.

- Medicare Part A—Covers hospitalization, skilled nursing facilities, and hospice care.

- Medicare Part B—Covers preventive care, primary care, outpatient care, and durable medical equipment.

- Medicare Part C—See Medicare Advantage Plan.

- Medicare Part D—Covers prescription drugs.

- Medicaid—A program that the federal and state governments have for people with low income and little property.

- Medicare HMO—A special senior government insurance.

- Medigap—A private insurance that pays for care that Medicare does not pay for.

- medicines—Things you take into your body to make you feel better.
- mental—Mind or thinking part of the brain.

N

- nutrients—Material in food that is used by the body.

O

- osteoporosis—Condition of having weak or brittle bones.
- outpatient—You get care at a hospital, but you don't stay there overnight.
- over-the-counter (OTC)—Medicines you can buy without a doctor's prescription, like aspirin, vitamins, and cough syrup.

P

- Pap smear—A procedure to test for cervical cancer in women.
- periodontitis—A dental condition of advanced gum disease that destroys the bones in your mouth and gum tissue.
- Primary Care Provider (PCP)—A doctor or nurse who helps you stay healthy and is there when you are sick. A PCP is the same as your "regular" doctor.
- pharmacist—A person who gives you the medicine that the doctor orders by writing a prescription. The pharmacist can help you with over-the-counter and other health supplies.
- physical exam—A doctor or healthcare provider will look you over and do tests such as blood or x-ray.
- pneumonia—An infection in the lung.
- premium—Set amount you pay to keep your health insurance. You usually pay this each month.

- prescription—An order from the doctor for a medicine that is written on a piece of paper.

- prostate—A gland in men that is shaped like a doughnut and is under the bladder. The gland makes fluid that carries the sperm during ejaculation. It gets bigger as a man ages and can cause problems with urinating and cancer.

R

- referral—When you are sent to another doctor or office for services or extra care that your regular doctor or your PCP cannot do.

- refills—A number written on the label of every prescription medicine telling you how many times you can get more of the medicine without asking the doctor or nurse.

S

- samples—Small doses of medicine that the doctor or nurse may give you when you are in the doctor's office or clinic.

- shots—Medicine that is given with a needle and syringe that will keep you from getting certain diseases.

- side effects—What the medicine does to your body other than what you are taking the medicine for.

- smoke detectors—A device that makes a loud noise when there is smoke from a fire.

- skilled nursing facility (SNF)—Called 'SNIFF'. A place to go when you no longer need hospital care but are too sick to go home. Also called a Nursing Home.

- Social Security—A federal government insurance program for working Americans. It pays for Medicare health insurance.

- specialty—Someone who has been trained to know one part or system of the body very well.

- STDs (Sexually transmitted diseases)—Diseases that can be passed through sex acts.

- stool—Bowel movement. Passing solid waste from the body.

- surgery—When a doctor makes an incision (cut) in the body to correct a health problem.

- syphilis—A disease that is given to another person during sex.

T

- tetanus—Lockjaw. An infectious disease that causes the person to die.

- tinnitus—Noise or ringing in the ears.

- therapy—The treatment of a disease or illness.

- tooth decay—Permanent damage to your teeth, such as cavities and caries.

- treatment—Done by a doctor or nurse with actions such as surgery or medicine.

U

- urgent care—Where you go for medical care when you get sick or injured and want to get care right away. You know that the illness is not an emergency and will not cause death or harm.

- urine—Pee.

Word List

V

- vaccines—Medicine that is given with a needle and syringe that will keep you from getting certain diseases.
- vitamins—Things found in food and used by the body.

What's In This Book From A to Z

176

What's In This Book From A to Z

What's In This Book From A to Z

What's In This Book From A to Z

W

People We Want to Thank

We thank the following people for their help with this book.

Gloria Andrew

Harriet Udin Aronow, Ph.D.

Mary Ann Blue, R.N., B.S.H.S.

Robert H. Brumfield, Jr., M.D.

Ruth E. Ditsch, R.N., B.A.

Cecilia C. Doak, M.P.H.

Consuelo S. Flores, B.S.

Moataz K. Giurgius, M.D.

Gino Hasler

Elizabeth Heck, M.S.W.

Lorré Hindman, R.N., B.S.N.

Jocelyn Jenkins-Bautista, G.N.P.

Neva Johnson, B.A.

Denis Kitayama, PharmD.

Ann Kuklierus, R.N.

Ruth P. Lewis, R.N.

Gloria Mayer, R.N., Ed.D.

Thomas R. Mayer, M.D.

Muriel Medina, Ph.D.

Juanita Melcom

Reneé J. Merolli, R.N., M.A.

Lynne Mumaw, R.N.

Phyllis V. Mumaw, B.S.

Cathy Murphree, R.N.

Anne Phillips

Mary Ann T. Railey, B.A.

Dolores Ramos, R.D.H.

Audrey Riffenburgh, M.A.

Marian Ryan, Ph.D.

Florence M. Schwab

Alan C. Schwartz, M.D.

Nicholas Scotto, P.T.

W. Edna Taylor

Rosemary C. Treacy, M.Ed.

Amelia Velasquez

Nancy Ann Whyte, B.A.

Julia Wittner

Notes

Notes

Other Books in the Series

ISBN 978-0-9720148-9-2
$12.95

What To Do
For Your Teen's Health

The teen years are hard on parents and teens. There are many things you can do to help your teen. At last, an easy-to-read, easy-to-use book written by 2 nurses. This book tells you:

- About the body changes that happen to teens.
- How to get ready for the teen years.
- How to talk with your teen.
- What you can do to feel closer to your teen.
- How to help your teen do well in school.
- All about dating and sex.
- How to keep your teen safe.
- The signs of trouble and where to go for help.

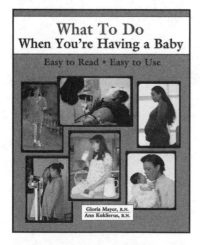

ISBN 978-0-9701245-6-2
$12.95

What To Do
When You're Having a Baby

There are many things a woman can do to have a healthy baby. Here's an easy-to-read, easy-to-use book written by 2 nurses that tells you:

- How to get ready for pregnancy.
- About the healthcare you need during pregnancy.
- Things you should not do when you are pregnant.
- How to take care of yourself so you have a healthy baby.
- Body changes you have each month.
- Simple things you can do to feel better.
- Warning signs of problems and what to do about them.
- All about labor and delivery.
- How to feed and care for your new baby.

Also available in Spanish.
To order, call (800) 434-4633 or visit www.iha4health.org.

Other Books in the Series

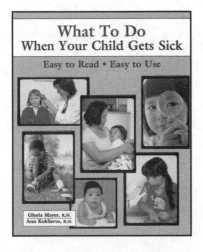

ISBN 978-0-9701245-0-0
$12.95

What To Do
When Your Child Gets Sick*

There are many things you can do at home for your child. At last, an easy-to-read, easy-to-use book written by 2 nurses.
This book tells you:

- What to look for when your child is sick.
- When to call the doctor.
- How to take your child's temperature.
- What to do when your child has the flu.
- How to care for cuts and scrapes.
- What to feed your child when he or she is sick.
- How to stop the spread of infection.
- How to prevent accidents around your home.
- What to do in an emergency.

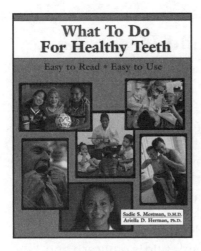

ISBN 978-0-9721048-0-9
$12.95

What To Do
For Healthy Teeth

It is important to take good care of your teeth from an early age. This book tells how to do that. It also explains all about teeth, gums, and how dentists work with you to keep your teeth healthy.

- How to care for your teeth and gums.
- What you need to care for your teeth and gums.
- Caring for your teeth when you're having a baby.
- Caring for your child's teeth.
- When to call the dentist.
- What to expect at a dental visit.
- Dental care needs for seniors.
- What to do if you hurt your mouth or teeth.

Also available in Spanish.
***Also available in Vietnamese.**
To order, call (800) 434-4633 or visit www.iha4health.org.

Other Books in the Series

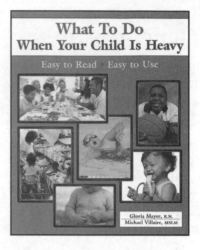

ISBN 978-0-9721048-4-7
$12.95

What To Do
When Your Child Is Heavy

There are many things you can do to help your heavy child live a healthy lifestyle. Here's an easy-to-read, easy-to-use book that tells you:

- How to tell if your child is heavy.
- How to shop and pay for healthy food.
- Dealing with your heavy child's feelings and self-esteem.
- How to read the Nutrition Facts Label.
- Healthy breakfasts, lunches and dinners.
- Correct portion sizes.
- Why exercise is so important.
- Tips for eating healthy when you eat out.
- Information on diabetes and other health problems of heavy children.

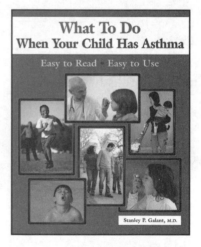

ISBN 978-0-9720148-6-1
$12.95

What To Do
When Your Child Has Asthma

Having a child with asthma can be scary. This easy-to-read, easy-to-use book tells you what you can do to help your child deal with asthma:

- How to tell if your child needs help right away.
- Signs that your child has asthma.
- Triggers for an asthma attack.
- Putting together an Asthma Action Plan.
- How to use a peak flow meter.
- The different kinds of asthma medicine.
- How to talk to your child's day care and teachers about your child's asthma.
- Making sure your child gets enough exercise.
- Helping your child to take asthma medicine the right way.
- What to do for problems such as upset stomach, hay fever and stuffy nose.

Also available in Spanish.
To order, call (800) 434-4633.